D0073441

Culture and Customs of Zimbabwe

Recent Titles in
Culture and Customs of Africa

Culture and Customs of Zimbabwe

∽∾

Oyekan Owomoyela

Culture and Customs of Africa
Toyin Falola, Series Editor

GREENWOOD PRESS
Westport, Connecticut • London

Library of Congress Cataloging-in-Publication Data

Owomoyela, Oyekan.
  Culture and customs of Zimbabwe / Oyekan Owomoyela.
     p.   cm.—(Culture and customs of Africa, ISSN 1530–8367)
  Includes bibliographical references and index.
  ISBN 0–313–31583–3 (alk. paper)
  1. Zimbabwe—Social life and customs.   2. Zimbabwe—Civilization.   I. Title.   II. Series.
DT2908.O86   2002
968.91—dc21   2001055647

British Library Cataloguing in Publication Data is available.

Library of Congress Catalog Card Number: 2001055647
ISBN: 0–313–31583–3
ISSN: 1530–8367

First published in 2002

Greenwood Press, 88 Post Road West, Westport, CT 06881
An imprint of Greenwood Publishing Group, Inc.
www.greenwood.com

Printed in the United States of America

The paper used in this book complies with the
Permanent Paper Standard issued by the National
Information Standards Organization (Z39.48–1984).

10 9 8 7 6 5 4 3 2 1

Contents

Photo essay follows page 74.

Series Foreword

AFRICA is a vast continent, the second largest, after Asia. It is four times the size of the United States, excluding Alaska. It is the cradle of human civilization. A diverse continent, Africa has more than fifty countries with a population of over 700 million people who speak over 1,000 languages. Ecological and cultural differences vary from one region to another. As an old continent, Africa is one of the richest in culture and customs, and its contributions to world civilization are impressive indeed.

Africans regard culture as essential to their lives and future development. Culture embodies their philosophy, worldview, behavior patterns, arts, and institutions. The books in this series intend to capture the comprehensiveness of African culture and customs, dwelling on such important aspects as religion, worldview, literature, media, art, housing, architecture, cuisine, traditional dress, gender, marriage, family, lifestyles, social customs, music, and dance.

The uses and definitions of "culture" vary, reflecting its prestigious association with civilization and social status, its restriction to attitude and behavior, its globalization, and the debates surrounding issues of tradition, modernity, and postmodernity. The participating authors have chosen a comprehensive meaning of culture while not ignoring the alternative uses of the term.

Each volume in the series focuses on a single country, and the format is uniform. The first chapter presents a historical overview, in addition to information on geography, economy, and politics. Each volume then proceeds to examine the various aspects of culture and customs. The series highlights the mechanisms for the transmission of tradition and culture across generations: the significance of orality, traditions, kinship rites, and family property distribution; the rise of print culture; and the impact of educational institutions. The series also explores the intersections between local, regional, national, and global bases for identity and social relations. While the volumes are organized nationally, they pay attention to ethnicity and language groups and the links between Africa and the wider world.

The books in the series capture the elements of continuity and change in culture and customs. Custom is not represented as static or as a museum artifact, but as a dynamic phenomenon. Furthermore, the authors recognize the current challenges to traditional wisdom, which include gender relations; the negotiation of local identities in relation to the state; the significance of struggles for power at national and local levels and their impact on cultural traditions and community-based forms of authority; and the tensions between agrarian and industrial/manufacturing/oil-based economic modes of production.

Africa is a continent of great changes, instigated mainly by Africans but also through influences from other continents. The rise of youth culture, the penetration of the global media, and the challenges to generational stability are some of the components of modern changes explored in the series. The ways in which traditional (non-Western and nonimitative) African cultural forms continue to survive and thrive, that is, how they have taken advantage of the market system to enhance their influence and reproductions also receive attention.

Through the books in this series, readers can see their own cultures in a different perspective, understand the habits of Africans, and educate themselves about the customs and cultures of other countries and people. The hope is that the readers will come to respect the cultures of others and see them not as inferior or superior to theirs, but merely as different. Africa has always been important to Europe and the United States, essentially as a source of labor, raw materials, and markets. Blacks are in Europe and the Americas as part of the African diaspora, a migration that took place primarily due to the slave trade. Recent African migrants increasingly swell their number and visibility. It is important to understand the history of the diaspora and the newer migrants, as well as the roots of the culture and customs of the places from where they come. It is equally important to understand others in order to be able to interact successfully in a world that keeps shrinking. The accessible nature of the books in this series will contribute to this understanding and enhance the quality of human interaction in a new millennium.

Toyin Falola
Frances Higginbothom Nalle
Centennial Professor in History
The University of Texas at Austin

Chronology

1888   Lobengula tricked into signing Rudd Concession giving Rhodes exclusive mining rights, which he later repudiates

1889   Rhodes's British South Africa Company (BSAC) formed andreceives Royal Charter

1890   BSAC's Pioneer Column of soldiers invades the territory and establishes Fort Salisbury; Witchcraft Suppression Act criminalizes purporting to practice witchcraft, accusing persons of practicing witchcraft, hunting witches, and soliciting persons to name witches

1891   Britain declares Bechuanaland, Matabeleland, and Mashonaland as protectorates

1892   Pass Laws enacted in Salisbury, controlling African presence in the city

1893   Ndebele War begins

1894   Death of Lobengula

1895   The territory is renamed Rhodesia

1896   Ndebele and Shona revolt; Ndebele revolt ends

1897   Shona revolt ends

1898   Kaguvi and Nehanda hanged

1901   Mapondera leads revolt; cattle fever begins

1902   Death of C. J. Rhodes

1923   Rhodesian Bantu Voters' Association formed; Rhodesia becomes crown colony

1925   Department of Native Education established

1929   Great Zimbabwe foundation excavated by the archeologist Gertrude Caton-Thompson; Ruwadzano organization (Methodist women's fellowship) formed

1930   Land Apportionment Act promulgated

1934   Bantu Congress (later African National Congress) formed by Aaron Jacha

1951   Native Land Husbandry Act promulgated

1953   Federation of Rhodesia and Nyasaland formed

1955   City Youth League founded (This is the more popular designation. It is also known as Southern Rhodesian African National Youth League.)

1956   Dominion Party (later Rhodesian Front) founded; first bus boycott in Salisbury organized by Youth League

1957   University College of Rhodesia and Nyasaland opens; African National Congress (ANC) formed

1959   State of emergency proclaimed; ANC banned; Unlawful Organisations Act passed

1960   National Democratic Party (NDP) formed; Kariba Dam opened

1961   Zimbabwe African People's Union (ZAPU) founded

1962   Rhodesian Front founded; ZAPU banned; Rhodesian Front wins national election

1963   Split in ZAPU ranks in Dar es Salaam; Zimbabwe African National Union (ZANU) founded; Federation of Rhodesia and Nyasaland dissolved

1964   Zimbabwe African National Liberation Army (ZANLA) formed by ZANU; Ian Smith becomes prime minister; Joshua Nkomo detained; ZANU banned; European settlers vote for independence

1965   ZAPU forms Zimbabwe People's Revolutionary Army (ZIPRA); Smith announces the Unilateral Declaration of Independence (UDI); Britain imposes economic sanctions

1966   Battle of Chinhoyi, first engagement of government forces by ZANLA

1967   ZAPU commences hostilities, in coordination with South Africa's ANC

1968   UN imposes comprehensive sanctions

1970   Rhodesia becomes a republic; Rhodesian Front sweeps elections

1971   ZANLA begins guerrilla warfare; Front for the Liberation of Zimbabwe (FROLIZI) formed; African National Council formed

1974   Robert Mugabe replaces Ndabaningi Sithole as leader of ZANU; Rhodesian Front sweeps general elections; ZANU, ZAPU, and FROLIZI accept ANC as umbrella organization; Smith announces agreement for cease-fire; Sithole, Nkomo, Mugabe, and others released from jail

1975   Smith, Nkomo, Abel Muzorewa, and Sithole meet to plan constitutional conference; Mozambique becomes independent;

Rhodesian government resumes anti-guerrilla fighting after cease-fire fails; South Africa withdraws its support for Rhodesia

1976   Smith meets U.S. Secretary of State Henry Kissinger in Pretoria; announces acceptance of idea of majority rule within two years; Nkomo and Mugabe form Patriotic Front

1977   Mugabe elected president of ZANU; Rhodesian front endorses majority rule; Organization of African Unity's Frontline States pledge support for Patriotic Front; both Britain and the United States follow suit and endorse ZANLA and ZIPRA as bases for independent Zimbabwe's army; Smith opens internal negotiations with Muzorewa, Sithole, and Jeremiah Chirau

1978   Smith rejects Anglo-American plan and signs Internal Agreement with Sithole, Muzorewa, and Chirau; amnesty announced for guerrillas who lay down their arms; ZANU and ZAPU bans lifted, but are soon reimposed

1979   Smith dissolves parliament; general elections held with Africans participating; Rhodesian Front candidates win all 28 white seats, while Muzorewa's United African National Council (UANC) wins 51 of 72 African seats; Britain's Conservative Party under Margaret Thatcher wins general elections; Muzorewa becomes Rhodesia's prime minister; Lancaster House Conference begins, with Muzorewa and Smith representing the Rhodesian government, and Mugabe and Nkomo representing the Patriotic Front; Rhodesia returns to colony status; cease-fire takes effect

1980   Mugabe and Nkomo return to the country; ZANU wins 57 out of 80 parliamentary seats in general election; Mugabe forms coalition government with ZAPU, with Nkomo as minister of home affairs; Mugabe is sworn in as prime minister of independent Zimbabwe; independence is declared on April 18; fighting erupts between former ZANLA and ZIPRA guerrillas in Bulawayo

1981   Mugabe announces intentions to create a one-party state; Mass Media Trust created

1982   Nkomo rejects Mugabe's plans to merge ZAPU with ZANU; arms cache discovered on farms owned by ZAPU members; Nkomo accused of plotting to overthrow the government and dismissed from the cabinet; government sends forces into Matabeleland

1983   Mozambique guerrillas attack Zimbabwe oil pipelines; Nkomo flees the country but returns later

1984   Remaining ZAPU members of government dismissed

1987   Smith resigns from parliament and retires from politics; post of prime minister abolished, and executive presidency created; Mugabe and Nkomo sign Unity Pact

1988   General amnesty is proclaimed for dissidents

1989   Edgar Tekere founds Zimbabwe Unity Movement

1990   Customary Law and Local Courts Act creates a unitary court system, comprising headmen's courts, chiefs' courts, magistrate courts, the High Court, and the Supreme Court

1992   Land Acquisition Act (Land Act) passed: amount of compensation for acquired farms can be appealed, but not the decision to acquire

1994   Supreme Court rules discriminatory and unconstitutional the law allowing men but not women to automatically confer residency rights on foreign-born spouses

1995   ZANU-PF (Patriotic Front) overwhelmingly wins parliamentary elections

1996   Mugabe easily wins reelection as president; bill passes disallowing both men and women to automatically confer citizenship rights on foreign-born spouses

1997   July: Foundation for Democracy in Zimbabwe established; Ndabaningi Sithole convicted and sentenced to two years in jail for conspiracy to kill Mugabe in 1995; the Administration of Estates Amendment Act removing inheritance laws unfavorable to women comes into effect; approximately 40 Non-Governmental Organizations (NGO's), labor unions, and political parties form the National Constitutional Association, advocating a new constitution that would limit the powers of the presidency; Mugabe appoints a 400-member Constitutional Commission to review the constitution; its December 11 report supports maintaining a strong presidency

1998   January: food riots over increases in the cost of basics like bread, maize meal, and cooking oil; October: National Constitutional Assembly demonstrates against intervention in the Democratic Republic of the Congo (DRC); November: protests and riots over imposition of 67 percent increase in price of gasoline and cooking oil; the University of Zimbabwe Amendment Act and National Council for Higher Education Act place universities under government control

1999   July 5: Nkomo funeral; December: Zimbabwe Confederation of Trade Unions launches the Movement for Democratic Change

2000   ZANU-PF barely wins national elections, beating off a strong challenge from the Movement for Democratic Change

2001   January: Mugabe rejects courts' right to order the government to compensate farmers for their seized farms; war veterans, with ZANU-PF backing, intensify their harassment of white farmers and their farm occupations; April: Mugabe announces his intention to run for the presidency in 2002, and the International Bar Association condemns Mugabe's government for causing a breakdown in law and order; June: the Rural Land Occupiers (Protection from Eviction) Act is signed into law; July: a 74 percent fuel price increase results in protest strike; in August the U.S. Senate passes the Zimbabwe Democracy Act calling for travel and economic sanctions on those responsible for the breakdown of law and order in the country; September: a Southern African Development Conference official declared Zimbabwe state-sponsored violence as adversely affecting the economy of the entire region

MOZAMBIQUE

ZAMBIA

Zambezi

Kariba

Lake
Kariba

NAMIBIA

Binga

Chinhoyi

HARARE

Chitungwiza

Hwange

Kadoma

Gweru

Mutare

Masvingo

Bulawayo

BOTSWANA

Beitbridge

MOZAMBIQUE

SOUTH AFRICA

0   100   200 km

0   100   200 mi

1

Introduction

THE COUNTRY OF ZIMBABWE enjoys a powerful mystique that attracts the world's attention, some of it due, no doubt, to its association with the Rider Haggard fictions *King Solomon's Mines* (1885) and *She* (1885) and the high level of international visibility it enjoyed during its years of notoriety as a land contested by white minority rulers and African freedom fighters. Other factors contributing to the attraction include the truly rich variety of sights and pleasures it offers visitors, the Great Zimbabwe ruins, Victoria Falls, and the world's largest concentration of ancient rock painting among them.

Zimbabwe, formerly known variously as Southern Rhodesia (1911–64), Rhodesia (1964–79), and Zimbabwe Rhodesia (1979–80), is a landlocked country in southern Africa, situated between the latitudes 15°33' south and 22°24' south, with a maximum length of 519 miles (835 km) and a width of 450 miles (725 km), and is situated entirely within the tropics. Covering an area of 150,873 square miles (390,759 sq km), it shares its boundary in the north with Zambia, in the northeast and east with Mozambique, in the south with South Africa, and in the southwest and west with Botswana; its extreme western corner touches Namibia. It is divided into eight administrative provinces: Manicaland in the east, Mashonaland East, Mashonaland Central, and Mashonaland West in the north, Matabeleland North in the west, Matabeleland South and Victoria in the south, and Midlands in the center.

A dominant feature of Zimbabwe's landscape is the Highveld, whose area constitutes a quarter of the country's land mass. The geological system of which it is a part dates back to between 190 and 345 million years ago, and includes the Drakensberg and Cape ranges in South Africa. This broad ridge lying between 4,000 and 5,000 feet (1,200–1,500 m) above sea level begins in the southwest and runs the length of the country, joining the Inyanga (Nyanga) and Chimanimani Mountains of the Eastern Highlands. It also forms a watershed from which streams drain into the Zambezi River at its northwestern end, and into the Limpopo and Save Rivers at the southeastern end. Over the millennia, erosion has resulted in the formation of wide plains with occasional deep valleys and outcrops known as kopjes, or koppies. The soils are generally thin and crumbly, and are easily susceptible to wind and water erosion. The most fertile parts lie at the northern end. The Highveld bisects the wide plateau of the Middleveld, whose elevation is between 2,000 and 4,000 feet (900–1,200 m), and which covers about two-fifths of the country's land surface. Here also the soil is poor, and erosion has exposed the underlying rocks in several places. The Lowveld, which lies in the southern part of the country, was formed from basaltic lavas and loose gravels, and is dotted with granites. It has an elevation ranging from 500 to 2,000 feet above sea level.

ZAMBEZI RIVER

The Zambezi (also spelled Zambesi, meaning "Great River" in the Tonga language) is the fourth largest river in Africa and one of the country's spectacular resources. It has its source on the Central African Plateau in the extreme northwest of Zambia and flows south through eastern Angola and western Zambia, entering Zimbabwe at Kazungula. From there it continues east, past Livingstone and the Victoria Falls, and then turns northeast, forming the man-made Kariba Lake, and marking the entire border between Zimbabwe and Zambia along its way. It enters Mozambique at Luangwa, near Kanyemba, and goes on to its mouth on the Indian Ocean. The Kariba Dam, located at Kariba Gorge, was completed in 1959 and has created Kariba Lake along the Zambia-Zimbabwe border. The lake is as wide as 25 miles (40 km) in some places and has a surface area of over 2,000 square miles (5,200 sq km), which makes it one of the largest man-made bodies of water in the world. Some distance beyond its western end toward the border with Namibia are the Victoria Falls, which, at approximately twice the width and twice the height of Niagara Falls, constitute one of the greatest natural wonders of the world.

FLORA

The variety and beauty of the country's flora so captivated an admirer that he described the land as a "wild garden of trees and aloes and flowering plants."[1] The vegetation is uniform over the country; bushveld, that is, thorny acacia (Wattle-like) savanna, and dry open woodland cover most of the western and central plateau, while the drier lowlands of the south and southeast support lower thorny scrub and baobabs (trees with huge trunks), as well as euphorbias (spurges), thirty species of aloes, poinsettia, jacarandas, hibiscus flame trees, bougainvilleas, jasmine, and a variety of citrus trees, palms, bananas, and perennials. Early European migrants and the paper industry planted pine forests, which now cover the higher slopes of the eastern highlands around Nyanga. On the eastern slopes of the Vumba are tropical hardwood forests, with vines and lianas (woody climbing plants), while tropical rainforests dominate the region close to the Victoria Falls.

FAUNA

The country is equally rich in animal life, and Zimbabwe has been able to exploit it to great advantage as a safari attraction. Several national parks scattered across the country are home to such creatures as elephants, buffalos, lions, a variety of large cats, monkeys, antelopes, and many more. Some species, among them the nyala (a kind of antelope) and the Samango monkey, are known to exist only in this country.

THE CLIMATE

Zimbabwe's location within the tropics, coupled with its high average elevation, gives it a subtropical climate. Its mean monthly temperatures are between 52 °F (11 °C) in July and 65 °F (18 °C) in October at Nyanga in the Inyanga Mountains in the east, while at Harare, on the Central Plateau, they range between 57 °F (14 °C) in July and 70 °F (21 °C) in October. The country enjoys four overlapping seasons: winter begins in May and lasts until August, followed by spring, which lasts until November. Summer starts in November and ends in April, and autumn spans April and May. During the winter months, little rain falls, and temperatures may drop below freezing at night. Winter and summer temperatures tend to be cooler in the Highveld and Eastern Highlands than in the Middleveld and Lowveld. The spring is warm and dry, but with summer comes the rainy season, during which precipitation occurs in intermittent, heavy downpours. At times the deluge is so heavy that all the water is wasted in runoffs, and the excess often wipes out a whole year's farm work in minutes. The Eastern Highlands have the highest rainfall, at about 40 inches (1,000 mm) annually; the amount decreases toward the southwest, where it averages about 16 inches (400 mm) in the Lowveld.

ECONOMY

Most Zimbabweans are farmers, and only a quarter of the country's population lives in cities. Most city-dwellers maintain social and economic links with their rural homelands. In precolonial times the people practiced shifting cultivation, moving seasonally to new farmlands as the old ones became exhausted, as did much of the rest of Africa. The system was so efficient that it not only satisfied their needs, but its products also helped sustain the early white settlers, and provided Africans with a source of income with which to pay the taxes the settlers levied on them.

The overwhelming predominance of agriculture persisted during the colonial period, until the imposition of economic sanctions on the Smith regime after its Unilateral Declaration of Independence (UDI) in 1965 forced the country to diversify. It developed and expanded local food processing and metal manufacture to make up for commodities it could no longer readily import, at the same time maximizing agricultural output and developing the service sector. The country produces some gold, nickel, and asbestos, and exports such agricultural products as cotton, tobacco, and maize, along with manufactured goods. Its gross domestic product (GDP) is well dispersed over several economic sectors, but the growth of the gross national product (GNP) lags behind that of the population, and per capita GNP remains relatively low by world standards, although it is well above the average for southern Africa.

After independence in 1980 the Mugabe government made a brief effort to adopt a one-party state and a Marxist economic system, but the collapse of the Eastern European economies that were based on the Marxist model undermined the effort. In addition, the failure of the mixed economy that prevailed during the first decade of independence forced the government to adopt an Economic Structural Adjustment Programme (ESAP).

Agriculture

An agreeable climate and good land, about two-thirds of which is suitable for cultivation, make for a healthy agricultural sector that enables Zimbabwe to be self-sufficient in foodstuffs. Nearly half of the country's population depends on subsistence agriculture, and up to 75 percent rely directly or indirectly on agriculture for a living. In addition, agriculture also provides about one-eighth of the GDP and accounts for about 30–40 percent of the country's total export earnings. Most of the agricultural products come from large plantations that are owned by whites, and that cover about half of the farm surface. The crops include corn (maize), sugarcane, wheat, groundnuts, sunflower seed, cotton, tobacco, sorghum, millet, and soybeans. The farms also produce high grade beef and dairy products, and lately, they have added coffee and tea to the complement of their commercial crops.

Black-owned farms mostly produce subsistence crops like corn, millet, peanuts, cassava, potatoes, dry beans, bananas, and oranges on their small holdings. A handful of white farmers still own most of the best arable lands, while Africans, the vast majority of the population, must make do with the poor land left over. This unequal distribution of land, a legacy of the racist colonial regimes, remains an almost intractable problem for the government two decades after independence.

Cattle

About one-eighth of the country's land area is devoted to rangeland and pastures for cattle, goats, and sheep. African pastoralists own about half of the cattle population, whose meat, milk, and skins are consumed in the subsistence economy and in social transactions such as bridal gift exchanges. Disputes surrounding livestock, specifically cattle, have plagued the European settlers' relations with Africans over the years. In the 1890s European settlers confiscated large numbers of Africans' animals, claiming them as spoils of war, and subsequent measures they took, ostensibly or actually to control rinderpest, further incensed the local population. The disputes were still very much alive during the armed struggle for independence.

Mineral Resources

Zimbabwe has abundant mineral reserves. The earliest Europeans were drawn to the region because of wild tales of the precious metal lying all over the land just for the picking. They turned out to be exaggerations. Gold is still plentiful being the most abundant of the mineral resources, followed by nickel and asbestos. Also available are coal, copper, chrome, iron ore, silver, and tin. Mining accounts for about one-twelfth of the GDP and employs about one-twentieth of the labor force.

Manufacturing

As noted above, the sanctions that followed the Smith regime's UDI gave a boost to manufacturing. The manufacturing sector now produces more than 25 percent of the GDP and employs about 16 percent of the labor force. Roughly half of the industrial capacity is devoted to agricultural products, the rest going to the processing of crude steel, pig iron and semi-manufactured steel, cement, electrical and other machinery, cotton textiles, clothing, footwear, chemicals, plastics, rubber products, fertilizers, and pesticides.

Communication and Utilities

Zimbabwe generates one-third of its electrical power from hydroelectric plants; at its commissioning in 1960 the Kariba Dam was the largest hydroelectric plant in the world. The balance of the electrical power comes from thermal plants. The government-operated railway system, which is about 10 percent electrified, extends some 1,700 miles (2,700 km) and is one of the most elaborate in sub-Saharan Africa. It is complemented by an extensive road system, about 20 percent of which is paved. There is an international airport at Harare as well as air service to the major urban centers.

Exports

Along with gold and ferrochrome, tobacco is one of the top foreign exchange generators; indeed, Harare is the home of the biggest tobacco auction floors in the world. The country also exports a substantial amount of good quality beef, and its cotton lint is ranked among the finest in the world. In addition, the newly developed horticulture sector exports huge quantities of vegetables and flowers. State interest in export is evident in such state establishments as the Cotton Marketing Board, which is responsible for cotton export; the Grain Marketing Board, which is responsible for grains, maize, and wheat; the Cold Storage Commission, which handles beef export; and the Dairy Marketing Board, which oversees milk products.

Post-Independence Horticulture and Tourism

The end to the fighting that led to independence has enabled the country to resume the exploitation of its many tourist attractions and to promote safaris. The best draws are the Great Zimbabwe ruins (a World Heritage), the Zimbabwe River, and Victoria Falls. Others are Lake Kariba, which many regard as one of the greatest engineering marvels of the twentieth century, and the rock art in such places as the Matobo National Park, Domboshawa and Ngomakurira (north of Harare), Mutoko, and elsewhere.

In general, state-owned monopolies dominate the nonfarm sector, where mismanagement, poor governance, and corruption are rife. The entire economy also suffers from the crippling effects of the government's military involvement in the Democratic Republic of the Congo (DRC) since 1998.

Great Zimbabwe National Monument

At Great Zimbabwe are found the remains of what is reputed to have been the greatest medieval city in sub-Saharan Africa. It was the religious and secular capital of a prosperous kingdom, and it held a population of between 10,000 and 20,000 people. According to historians, over 150 tributaries (*zimbabwes*) constituted the Great Zimbabwe society, in effect an amalgamation of several smaller groups. The name Zimbabwe is believed to derive from one of two possible Shona origins: either *dzimba dza mabwe* (great stone houses) or *dzimba woye* (esteemed houses).[2] Although skeptics long doubted that an African people could have erected the structures, their Bantu origin was established by 1932, thanks to the investigations and findings of the British archeologist Gertrude Caton-Thompson.

CITIES

Harare

Harare, with a population of about 1.6 million, is the capital and the largest city in the country, as well as a commercial and main economic center. It was founded as Fort Salisbury on September 12, 1890, when Major Frank Johnson, leader of the Pioneer Column of the British South African Company, planted the Union Jack in the flats located in the northeast of the Central Plateau. Until then the location was the seat of Chief Neharawa of Seki (now Seke). Johnson named the new settlement in honor of Lord Salisbury, the British prime minister at the time, but the settlers named a section of it Harare, derived from Harawa, the name the Africans preferred to use for the area. Salisbury officially became the capital of Southern Rhodesia in 1923, but at independence its name was changed to Harare, affirming the Africans' preference. The city experienced considerable growth after World War II, when it became the capital of the Federation of the Rhodesias and Nyasaland, a status that enabled it to siphon resources from the other two countries in the federation for its own benefit. It established its industrial base during this period, and although it virtually stagnated after UDI, independence has brought about a renaissance.

Harare, with its tall glass buildings, fast-food restaurants, and Western-style clothing shops and boutiques, as well as the older structures dating to the colonial era, is not a typical African city. Rather, it is a thriving modern city with a distinctly European character, not surprising given its history. It is also the focus of Zimbabwe's cultural life, characterized by the bustle one would expect at the confluence of multiple currents and activities. The main international airport is located here, as are the foreign embassies, the University of Zimbabwe, the National Archives, the National Gallery, and the Queen Victoria Museum, not to mention various architectural and arboreal monuments and attractions.

The legacy of the colonial period persists in the segregation of the rich from the poor, the former living in posh suburbs while the latter live in working-class enclaves. Mbare, with its huge bustling market and bus station, is the African city in the midst of Harare.

Bulawayo

Bulawayo was founded in 1871 by King Lobengula, who succeeded Mzilikazi the previous year. It is the capital and principal city of Matabeleland, the Ndebele area of the country. With a population of close to 1 million inhabitants, it is the country's second largest city and a major commercial center. Its name, which means "Place of Slaughter" in Ndebele, is a testimony to the bloody battles that raged in the area in the nineteenth century. Lobengula made it his seat until he set it alight and fled north to escape British troops in 1893. Leander Starr Jameson, the leader of the British forces, occupied the city and erected the Government House at the site of Lobengula's home. On June 1, 1894, he proclaimed the official founding of the new city, but retained the name of the old.

On its establishment, the new city enjoyed a surge in population as a result of a gold rush, and in 1898 Cecil Rhodes's Cape-to-Cairo railway arrived; Bulawayo soon outstripped Fort Victoria (now Masvingo) as the country's main communication hub, linking Salisbury (Harare) with South Africa. Today, the headquarters of the National Railways is located in the city, which also holds such other attractions as the Museum of Natural History (featuring indigenous wildlife as well as artifacts), the Railway Museum, and the Mabukuwene Nature Reserve.

Bulawayo is more interesting than Harare because its colonial-era architectural heritage has escaped the demolition ball that has been busy in Harare. It is more conservative and slower-paced than the capital city, and is also blessed by its nearness to the Matopo Hills and Matobo National Park with its prehistoric rock paintings. Being the home base of Joshua Nkomo, Bulawayo and Matabeleland were subjected to murderous raids by government forces in the internecine fighting that broke out after independence. A Unity Accord signed in 1988 cemented a reconciliation, and a second university has been sited in Bulawayo as part of the strategy to placate the Ndebele.

Chitungwiza

This satellite city, located to the southeast of Harare, south of Harare International Airport, developed after independence to ease congestion in the capital. Its establishment dates to 1977, when a government proclamation authorized it as a separate urban area. With a population of nearly a million, it is in effect Zimbabwe's third largest city.

Gweru

Known as Gwelo until 1982, the city was founded in 1894 in a gold mining area, and is conveniently located between Bulawayo and Harare. It is today a goods transit center and an industrial and commercial hub linked by rail with cities in South Africa and Mozambique and within Zimbabwe itself. Its attractions include the Midlands Museum (which houses such military hardware as guns, warplanes, grenades, and the like from the world wars) and Antelope Park.

Other Cities

Other major urban centers include Mutare (formerly Umtali), Kwe Kwe (formerly Que Que), and Masvingo (formerly Fort Victoria).

POPULATION

The population of a little over 11 million people is 71 percent Shona, 16 percent Ndebele, 11 percent other, 1 percent mixed and Asian, and less than 1 percent white. The San, nomadic hunter-gatherers, were the earliest human inhabitants of Zimbabwe, Botswana, and Namibia, and are responsible for the wealth of rock paintings found all over the area. Between A.D. 500 and 1000 the ancestors of today's dominant population, Bantu-speaking agriculturalists of the Gokomere culture, began arriving in the cool, temperate higher elevations of Zimbabwe. They took to rearing cattle, and traded in gold and ivory. Today, the country's population is largely homogenous, unlike many African countries that are an amalgam of several distinct ethnic groups.

Shona

Of the African population, the dominant ethnolinguistic group is the Shona (comprising the subgroups Karanga, Zezuru, Manyika, Tonga-Korekore, Rowzi, and Ndau), at 71 percent of the total population. Their language, Shona, is relatively ancient and diverse, each of the constituent groups having its own variant; the six main dialects are divided into over thirty minor ones, with Zezuru enjoying a privileged status, because it is spoken in Harare and on the radio.

The Shona migrated into the area in the tenth and eleventh centuries from the Shaba region of the Congo and soon became the most powerful inhabitants. They erected the Great Zimbabwe stone fortress as their capital and a shrine to Mwari, their supreme deity. From there they traded with the Swahili on the coast of modern-day Mozambique, exchanging gold and ivory for glass, porcelain, and cloth from Asia. They live mainly in the eastern parts of the country, north of the Lundi River, their villages being composed of huts and granaries built of pole and *daga* (plaster made from termite hills), and nearby kraals (enclosures) for the community's cattle. They are patrilineal for the most part, but some northern branches (like the Tonga) are matrilineal, descent passing through the female line, and chieftaincies are hereditary. They believe in one creator, Mwari, and hold the propitiation of ancestors crucial, since their involvement in human affairs is intimate, and such things as rainfall and the health and prosperity of the living depend on their good humor. The Shona communicate with their ancestors and other spirits through mediums, and maintain a strong belief in magic, sorcery, and witchcraft.

The Shona are predominantly farmers, growing millet, sorghum, and corn (maize), the main constituent of their staple food, *sadza* (a kind of porridge). In addition, they cultivate rice, beans, peanuts, and sweet potatoes. They also keep cattle, which supply them with milk, but most especially act as status symbols and means of exchange, as bride-price for example. Traditionally, they achieved considerable expertise as ironworkers and potters, and still enjoy a good reputation as musicians.

Ndebele

The Ndebele (and its subgroup the Kalanga) come next to the Shona in numbers, accounting for 16 percent of the population. They are Nguni-speaking pastoralists who under Mzilikazi (Moselekatse), commander of Chaka's armies during the *mfecane* (forced migrations) of the 1820s and 1830s, also known by the Sotho word *difaqane* (the crushing), defected and fled north, settling in the vicinity of modern-day Bulawayo. The Matabele kingdom Mzilikazi founded comprised hereditary chieftainships related to him by kin, and independent ones that paid tribute to him and to Lobengula, his successor. Apart from Zimbabwe, where their capital city is Bulawayo, they are also to be found in northern South Africa and eastern Botswana. Their language and Zulu are mutually intelligible.

From the start the Ndebele interacted with their Shona neighbors by raiding their cattle, but also intermarrying with them and absorbing some of their villages. They also adopted the Shona cult of Mwari as well as its medium culture. They grow maize and other subsistence crops on their farms, and also engage in cattle rearing.

Other African Groups

The Balonka, Shangane, and Venda make up the balance of the African population.

Whites

Cecil John Rhodes's imposition of the British South African Company (BSAC) control and the proclamation of British protectorate over the area in 1891 led to an influx of whites. Their exploitation and mistreatment of the African population form much of the recent history of the country (which is discussed below). Many whites abandoned the country on the approach of independence, the remnants constituting a little over 1 percent of the population.

PREHISTORY

The earliest inhabitants, since around 8000 B.C. were the San, who subsisted by gathering and hunting with bows and stone-tipped arrows. They lived in extended family groups and are widely believed to have created the sophisticated rock paintings widespread over the area, depicting religious and ritual scenes involving humans and animals. They were eventually supplanted and absorbed by Khoi-Khoi pastoralists. The new group was linguistically related to the San (hence Khoisan), and historians attribute the introduction of farming and a sedentary lifestyle (which was well established by 200 B.C.) to the Khoisan; they remained dominant into the sixteenth century. These inhabitants developed a civilization that lasted from about A.D. 100 to about 1500. The extent of the kingdom amazed the first European visitor, the Portuguese Antonio Fernandes, who arrived there in 1514 during his second and more extensive journey in the area. (The first was in about 1511.)

Bantu-speaking migrants skilled in the use of iron tools and weapons began migrating into the area in waves before A.D. 300 and continuing until the beginning of the second millennium. The first were the Gokomere, agriculturalists and ironworkers, who established themselves in the cool savanna highlands in the vicinity of the Great Zimbabwe site, which had the advantage of being easily defensible. The lineage heads owned large herds of cattle, the size determining the wealth and authority of the owner. Cattle ranching became the main occupation, but the people also mined gold and produced good quality ceramics, jewelry, soapstone carvings, and textiles.

GREAT ZIMBABWE

The presumed ancestors of the Shona, probably several groups that banded together for safety, were in place in the area by the eleventh century. Among the last immigrants, they lived in huts constructed of poles and plaster, and coexisted peacefully with earlier occupants of the area and their cultures, which they never completely displaced. They soon established their dominance, though, not by force but through superior organization. Thereafter they constructed stone structures (*dzimbawhe*), royal courts (or royal stone residences), the largest being the Great Zimbabwe seventeen miles (27 km) east of present-day Masvingo in the Mtilikwe basin in the south-central part of the country. It is about 155 miles (250 km) south of the capital, Harare. It sprawls over an expanse of almost 1,800 acres, in an open woodland encircled by hills, and at its most influential it was home to over 10,000 inhabitants, with between 200 and 300 residents living within the stone walls. Its magnificence so impressed the first Europeans to see it that they sought to attribute its construction to non-Africans. The speculations and suppositions seemed in order, especially because the Europeans detected no great stone workmanship among the people they found, and the Shona, in spite of their long and continuous presence in the area, could provide no account of the origins and history of the structures. Up until the time of independence even the Rhodesian government subscribed to theories supporting foreign influence, although by 1932 archeological investigations had established beyond any doubt that the construction was the work of an indigenous African people.

Historians and archeologists believe that the complex, comprising the Hill Ruins or Hill Complex, the Western (or Great) Enclosures, and the Valley Ruins, was a royal city built between the eleventh and fifteenth centuries by the Rozvi (or Rozwi) ancestors of the modern-day Shona, who maintained their royal enclosure within the Hill Complex. As the heart of the Rozwi culture, the city held ever-increasing royal herds and hoards of treasures. Objects uncovered by diggers at the site include tools for working metals (iron, copper, and gold), copper bracelets and ceremonial weapons, several other objects in gold and copper, stone platters, and earthenware. Also included were tools and instruments suggesting cotton-related activities. The Hill Complex is believed to have later been the home of a Rozwi spirit medium. In one of the enclosures is a natural cave that echoes voices to the valley below, giving rise to speculation that it was once the home of an oracle; hence the frequent reference to it as the "Acropolis."

The royal enclosures on the Hill Complex, which is located on a 330 ft (c.100 m) high kopje to the north of the site, were built first, the construction beginning in the thirteenth century. The Western Enclosures lie in the plains about 1,980 ft (600 m) due south of the Hill Complex. The Elliptical

Building, which is also sometimes called the Temple, the Great Enclosure, and so forth, is located here; it was one of the later structures to be built and is believed to have been the most important in the complex, but its original function remains a mystery. The extensive expansions to the Great Zimbabwe during the fourteenth century testify to a significant improvement in building techniques, which continued into the first part of the fifteenth century, when the latest and most refined construction took place on the stone walls.

The imposing exterior walls were obviously not built to support roofs, and investigators believe that they served no defensive function and offered only limited privacy. They conclude, consequently, that they were simply a means of proclaiming the prestige of the ruler, one capable of marshaling the manpower, skills, and resources to erect such a monument. Several other rulers followed the Rozvi lead; consequently, as many as 200 zimbabwes dot the area between the Zambesi and the Limpopo, each testifying to a royal presence, but none is as magnificent as the Great Zimbabwe. Venda chiefs continued to build zimbabwes up to the late twentieth century, where members of the royal lineage surmount their walls with monoliths to commemorate their ancestors. Lately they have substituted wood staves for the monoliths. Their huts continued to be of pole-and-plaster construction, and allocation of space within the capital was made according to a hierarchy, the highest spot being reserved for the chief and his wives.

The inhabitants of the Great Zimbabwe engaged in agriculture and owned a wealth of cattle. In addition, they traded in gold and copper with the Swahili, who had been plying the coast of modern-day Mozambique since the time of the Zanj Empire (tenth century), and continued to do so through the height of Rowzi influence in the fourteenth and fifteenth centuries. They also sold ivory, much in demand in India because it was easier to carve into trinkets and bracelets than the hard and brittle Indian variety. In return they received glass beads, cloth, and porcelain. Their armies protected the trade, and they extracted tolls whose proceeds contributed to the building of the Great Zimbabwe. But by the fifteenth century its influence was in decline, probably owing to overpopulation, overgrazing, land exhaustion, and internal conflict. Another view, though, is that the decline was probably part of a widespread process, including the decline of East African trading cities and of other Shona states—the Mutapa and the Khami. In any case, by the end of the sixteenth century, when the first Portuguese arrived, the site was deserted.

MWENE MUTAPA

The Mutapa dynasty that emerged from the disintegration of the Great Zimbabwe was a loose federation that established itself in northern and eastern Zimbabwe, under *mambo* (king) Mutota Nyatsimba (d. 1450), who was known as Mutapa Mutota and Mwene Mutapa ("the great raider"). The last name is variously rendered as Munhumutapa, Munomutapa, Mwana-mutapa, and Monomotapa. He ruled democratically and by consensus, and trained carefully selected young men at his court to serve later as ambassadors, counselors, lords, and so forth. The seat of his empire at Zvongombe was closer to the gold fields and the coast, and was thus better positioned for the gold trade.

EUROPEANS AND THE LURE OF GOLD

Vasco da Gama and his crew landed at Sofala in 1502 and were besotted by the mouth-watering tales they heard from Arab traders about the gold riches of Monomotapa, which were confirmed by Arab dhows laden with gold dust at the mouth of the Zambezi. A Portuguese visitor wrote home in 1520, "In the realms of Munomutapa gold is almost . . . common. Besides his own central kingdom, which lies inland from Sofala, the Benomptapa is Emperor over many vassals who pay tribute in gold, his rule stretches almost to the Cape of Good Hope."[3] The Europeans publicized reports at home to the effect that gold could be had aplenty just for the picking, without the need of hammers or other tools, as it covered the land as far as the eyes could see.

By 1505 the Portuguese had managed to establish their control along the coast, where they engaged in direct barter trading with the Mutapa people. They attempted to subjugate the Mutapa but failed; before long, however, rivalry among the ruling elite did what the Portuguese could not do on their own. They were thus able in 1629 to convert the peaceful trading arrangement to one in which they could impose their sway. It lasted only until 1663, though, when they were expelled by an alliance of Changa (Mutapa Mutota's grandson) and the Rozvi Changamire, who had succeeded the Torwa state to the west a century earlier. The Rozvi then subjugated the Mutapa, and remained ascendant into the nineteenth century, when events in the south led to developments that ended Shona rule and independence.

THE *MFECANE*

Chaka's fearsome military campaigns to the south both created a powerful Zulu nation and caused other groups to flee to distant lands beyond his army's reach, in what is known in history as the *difaqane* or *mfecane* (forced migration). In 1822 an Nguni group fled north across the Limpopo under Mzilikazi (Moselekatse), once a commander of Chaka's armies, and in 1838 arrived in the vicinity of present-day Bulawayo, near the Matopo Hills.

There Mzilikazi founded the Ndebele state, Matabeleland, with its capital at Nyati. It incorporated several ethnic groups, including Zulu, Nguni, Sotho, Tswana, and Shona. From Inyati the Ndebele mounted cattle raids into the surrounding Shona territory, thus provoking the fear and resentment of the more numerous but less bellicose Shona.

RHODES AND THE RUDD CONCESSION

The London Missionary Society's Robert Moffat and his son John established a mission at Inyati in 1859 with Mzilikazi's blessings. On the latter's death in 1868 his son Lobengula became king and moved the Ndebele capital to Bulawayo, just as the European discovery of the Great Zimbabwe and reports of an abundance of gold were kindling intense European interest in the area. One of the most interested was Cecil John Rhodes, an English entrepreneur and adventurer who had grown rich from mining diamonds at Kimberley. His interest in the territory was kindled by the belief that it held abundant gold reserves, in addition, of course, to the facts that it lay in the path of his dream of a Cape-to-Cairo railway through a continuous band of territory owned by the British, and that its annexation would block any attempt at northward movement by the Afrikaners, who were giving the British some trouble to the south.

To further this aim, Rhodes dispatched Charles Rudd, accompanied by Robert Maguire and Frank Thompson, on a mission to Lobengula to seek permission for British exploration and prospecting on his land. The astute king smelled mischief and proved far cleverer than the Englishmen expected. The negotiations went on for months, during which, as Thompson reported, Lobengula "was as sharp as a needle. . . . He remembered everything and if you did contradict yourself, he was down on you at once."[4] In the end, Reverend Charles Helms, a cleric Lobengula trusted, came to the aid of Rhodes's men. Helms was born at the Cape, where he joined the London Missionary Society. He had a remarkable facility with languages and spoke Shona fluently. He arrived at Lobengula's court in 1875, and the king took him into his service, reposing great trust in him. Rhodes also enlisted John Moffat's help in getting the king's signature on a document, any document, and with Helms's connivance the king signed the infamous Rudd Concession of 1888, which granted Rhodes mining and colonization rights over Matabeleland.

FROM GOLD QUEST TO AGRICULTURE

The following year, Rhodes obtained a charter from the British crown creating the BSAC to, in effect, colonize and exploit the territory's minerals. In

1890 he dispatched soldiers known as the Pioneer Column into Shona territory to consolidate his hold. Avoiding direct conflict with Lobengula, they
raised the British flag over Fort Victoria (Masvingo) on June 27, at Fort Salisbury in September, and later at Umtali (Mutare), in the process staking
out farmlands in the highlands. In 1893 Leander Starr Jameson, the BSAC
administrator of the territory, seized the occasion of a punitive raid Lobengula's forces mounted against the Shona as an opportunity to impose
BSAC's undisputed authority. He construed the raid as an attack on the
BSAC and moved against the king, routed his army, and forced him to flee
into the wilderness, where he died the following year.

The "pacified" Ndebele quietly submitted to British rule for a while, and
a stream of European settlers poured into the country, hoping to make their
fortunes in gold. In time the Shona suffered the same fate as the Ndebele.
On top of these abuses the whites imposed a "hut tax" on Africans as a device to force them to seek employment at slave wages with the settlers.

Disappointed in their quest for gold, the deposits having long been de-
pleted, the pioneers took up farming and ranching, stealing the land from the
Ndebele with the authority of the BSAC. It gave the whites the so-called
White Highlands, the land lying north and south of the main road and railway between Harare and Butare, which, with its good rainfall and drainage,
comprised the best arable land on the high plateau. The BSAC pushed most
of the African population into the parched, tsetse-infested, and less desirable
Middleveld and Lowveld areas called Native Reserves, later Tribal Trust
Lands, and still later Communal Areas. There they could grow only a narrow
range of crops, mostly maize, and had no opportunities for capital accumula-
tion. The settlers also appropriated the people's cattle, which they argued
were spoils of war since they belonged to Lobengula.

In 1894 the BSAC promulgated an order-in-council that appointed an
administrator to control African affairs and empowered him to, among
other things, amalgamate different peoples who had little in common. The
following year the British named their new acquisition Rhodesia.

THE FIRST WAR OF LIBERATION

These and other provocations prompted the Ndebele, in concert with the
Shona, to rise in 1896 in what is known as the first war of liberation
(*chimurenga*) against Rhodes and his company. The Shona aspect of the in-
surrection effectively ended in 1897 with the capture and hanging of its
leaders, the *mhondoro* (mediums) Nehanda Charwe Nyakasikana, a woman,
and Sekuru Kaguvi. Nehanda's dying words were "My bones will rise
again," a cry celebrated much later in Chenjerai Hove's novel *Bones*. The

Ndebele *impis* (warriors) for their part fought on from their refuge in the Matopo Hills until an *indaba* (council) was arranged to conclude a peace which returned some of the land to them along with their autonomy. The BSAC ruled the territory, renamed Southern Rhodesia in 1899 to distinguish it from Northern Rhodesia (later Zambia), until British annexation made it a crown colony in 1923.

After the crushing of the first *chimurenga* the Southern Rhodesia government became more repressive. It formulated the Order-in-Council of 1898 and the Southern Rhodesia Native Regulations, which required Africans to register with colonial officials, the Native Commissioners. Africans were made to carry passes at all times, and any violation of the requirement was punishable by fines, imprisonment, or consignment to labor camps. These regulations remained in effect until after World War II.

DISENFRANCHISEMENT

The white settlers' exploitation of Africans continued. When the whites voted in 1923 by a margin of 8,774 to 5,783 to opt for self-government rather than join South Africa as its fifth province, the crown took over the administration of the colony from the BSAC. The Colonial Office established a whites-only parliament, and two years later the Carter Commission (headed by Andrew Carter) recommended a strict segregation of Europeans and Africans in the colony. Accordingly the British government passed the Land Apportionment Act of 1930. It remained in force until it was superceded by the Land Tenure Act of 1969. This later act gave exactly half of the land to whites, numbering about one quarter of a million, and the other half to Africans, totaling almost 5 million people, who were concentrated into infertile Native Reserves (later Tribal Trust Lands). They also instituted the *chibaro* (forced labor), which forced Africans to work for low wages in the mines.

Moreover, the colony's constitution disenfranchised Africans, basing suffrage on British citizenship and a level of income beyond Africans' reach. The whites were on the other hand able to set up huge farms which they financed with generous bank loans and worked with cheap African labor, especially as a 1934 labor law excluded Africans from skilled trades or labor, as well as from living in "white areas," which included all towns and cities.

FORMS OF RESISTANCE

During the 1920s and 1930s Africans formed resistance organizations such as the Rhodesian Bantu Voters' Association, the Southern Rhodesia Native

Association, and the Southern Rhodesia African National Congress. The people involved were eligible voters from the middle class, who were more interested in reformation than in revolution. In 1947 Benjamin B. Burombo formed the African Voice Association, which is regarded as the forerunner of the nationalist associations, and whose effectiveness is attested by its prohibition in 1952 under the provisions of the Subversive Activities Act of 1950. Worsening economic conditions in the 1940s occasioned the passage of the Native Land Husbandry Act of 1951, which allocated tiny plots of pasture land in the Native Reserves to African families, effectively forcing them to reduce their herd sizes.

FEDERATION

From 1952 to 1963 Southern Rhodesia joined Northern Rhodesia and Nyasaland in the "partnership" officially known as the Federation of Rhodesia and Nyasaland. The prime minister of the federation (from 1953 to 1956), Godfrey Huggins (formerly prime minister of Southern Rhodesia from 1933 to 1953), spoke of it as a partnership with the Africans which mimicked the relationship between a horse and its rider, the Europeans being the rider, of course, and the Africans the horse. The arrangement worked to the advantage of the white settlers of Southern Rhodesia, as it enabled them to appropriate the earnings from Northern Rhodesia's copper for developing their part of the federation. There was some slight improvement in the plight of the Africans, though, because pressure from the British government made the local government ease some of the restrictions on African employment, even though the whites would not contemplate political concessions.

In 1955 militant nationalists in Salisbury formed the City Youth League, whose merger with the Southern Rhodesia African National Congress in 1957 resulted in the creation of the African National Congress (ANC) under Joshua Nkomo's leadership. Banned in 1959, the ANC transformed itself into the National Democratic Party (NDP), but it too was banned in 1959, only to reemerge in 1961 as the Zimbabwe African People's Union (ZAPU). It fared little better than its earlier incarnations, as it was eventually proscribed, along with all African assemblies and political activities. Disputes on tactics caused a rift in the organization, leading to the dismissal of some malcontents, including Ndabaningi Sithole, Robert Mugabe, and Leopold Takawira. They reacted by forming their own association, the Zimbabwe African National Union (ZANU), on August 8, 1963.

The Federation of Rhodesia and Nyasaland collapsed in 1963; Northern Rhodesia became the independent nation of Zambia the following year, and Nyasaland emerged as independent Malawi. In Rhodesia the continued squabbling between ZAPU and ZANU gave the government an excuse to ban both parties and imprison their leaders.

The British government would not grant independence to the whites of Southern Rhodesia as long as they maintained a blatantly racist system. Accordingly, in December 1965 the defiant Ian Smith, who had become the leader of the Rhodesian Front the previous year, proclaimed the Unilateral Declaration of Independence (UDI) of Rhodesia in defiance of Britain. The British government refused to use force against its kith and kin to bring them back into the fold, but imposed sanctions on the renegade country, and the United Nations followed suit in 1968. The Smith regime could, however, count on the active support of South Africa and of the Portuguese and their Mozambican colony, and Rhodesia was therefore able to shrug off the sanctions, which most Western countries and even some British companies ignored anyway. The government also turned the sanctions to economic advantage, imposing import controls, encouraging domestic production, and promoting investment in the local market and industry.

THE SECOND *CHIMURENGA*

Meanwhile, in the face of Ian Smith's vow that "never in a thousand years" would Africans come to power in the country, they had taken up arms in 1966, and April 28 of that year saw the inauguration of the second *chimurenga*, a guerrilla campaign to oust the settlers. ZANU was the first to engage with its combat wing, the Zimbabwe National Liberation Army (ZANLA), but it was largely ineffective until Frelimo (the Mozambique liberation front) successes in neighboring Mozambique enabled it to operate from the liberated areas of that country. ZAPU went into alliance with South Africa's ANC and formed a military wing, the Zimbabwe People's Revolutionary Army (ZIPRA), which trained in Tanzania and operated from bases in Zambia.

In 1969, under guerrilla attack and pressure from the British, Smith's regime offered a constitution that would have guaranteed eight seats in a parliament of sixty-six to Africans, but, largely thanks to a vigorous campaign in which Bishop Abel Muzorewa played a prominent role, it was rejected. The bishop was to feature in a less glorious light ten years later, when in the service of Smith's "internal settlement" he agreed to lead a puppet African government that Smith effectively controlled.

RACISM'S LAST THROES

The year 1974 was an eventful one for Zimbabwe. In April a coup in Lisbon toppled the Portuguese government and ushered in independence for Angola and Mozambique, suddenly exposing the Smith regime's flanks along those borders, and causing both South Africa (also exposed to a hostile, independent Mozambique) and the United States, both effective supporters of the Smith regime, to rethink their position. Within the country the nationalist groups united under the umbrella of the African National Congress on December 8, with Bishop Abel Muzorewa as its leader. At a meeting on the Zambezi Bridge at Victoria Falls attended by John Vorster of South Africa and Kenneth Kaunda of Zambia, Ian Smith yielded to pressure to release Nkomo, Sithole, Mugabe, and other freedom fighters from jail.

Disagreements between Muzorewa and Nkomo on tactics led to the latter's expulsion from the ANC, and ZANU also saw a change in leadership, with Mugabe replacing Sithole. On October 9, 1976, Mugabe and Nkomo joined forces to form the Patriotic Front, and the military wings of their organizations, ZANLA and ZIPRA, combined to form ZIPU (Zimbabwe People's Army). Confronted with these developments, Ian Smith sought an "internal settlement" that he hoped would quell African agitation while leaving his minority regime in power. He succeeded in persuading Sithole and Muzorewa to join him in a transitional arrangement based on a guarantee of 28 seats to whites in a parliament of 100. The whites would also enjoy veto powers over all legislation for the next ten years, their property would be inalienable, and they would control the security forces, the judiciary, and the civil service. The African nationalists responded with an intensification of their military activities.

Smith's next gambit was to offer to call a general election. He dissolved the parliament on February 28, 1979, and despite objections from Britain and the United States went ahead with elections open to all races for the first time. Predictably, the Rhodesian Front won all twenty-eight seats reserved for whites and Muzorewa's UANC won fifty-one of the seventy-two seats reserved for Africans. On May 1, 1979, Smith installed Muzorewa as prime minister of Zimbabwe-Rhodesia, Muzorewa's acquiescence effectively destroying whatever esteem the bishop had remaining from his earlier nationalistic activities. In any case, Smith's moves did not substantially alter the political reality, the existing social and economic structures, or international disapproval of the situation in the country.

When Margaret Thatcher's government assumed power in Great Britain in 1979, it embarked on new, serious efforts to resolve the Rhodesian impasse by means of an acceptable constitution and a credible election. It convened the Lancaster House Conference in London on September 10 for the purpose, which the principals on both sides attended: Smith and Muzorewa for the Rhodesia-Zimbabwe government, and Mugabe and Nkomo for the Patriotic Front. Also participating were Tanzania's Julius Nyerere, Zambia's

Kenneth Kaunda, and, of course, Great Britain's Margaret Thatcher. After much wrangling they agreed on a constitution that guaranteed 20 seats to the white settlers in a parliament of 100, and also protected their land holdings, which could not be taken from them without adequate compensation.

ELECTION AND INDEPENDENCE

A new election took place on March 4, 1980; ZANU won fifty-seven of the eighty black seats, ZAPU took twenty-seven, and UANC (Muzorewa's party) captured three, even though South Africa had pumped considerable amounts of money into Muzorewa's campaign, because it regarded the pliable bishop as someone who would not interfere with apartheid in South Africa. Mugabe thus became the prime minister of independent Zimbabwe, and the Reverend Canaan Banana was sworn in as president on April 16.

Although a committed Marxist, Mugabe accepted the advice of President Samora Marchel of Mozambique, who counseled against expelling or frightening off the whites. He adopted a moderate and conciliatory policy, which included offering some cabinet positions to whites and including Nkomo in the cabinet. He thus reassured the whites and the international community, and the economy prospered.

DESTABILIZATION AND SQUABBLES

Renamo (Mozambican national resistance movement), originally created in the 1970s by Rhodesia to harass Mozambique, now launched attacks from its base in South Africa on the railway from Rhodesia to Maputo and Beira in order to force Zimbabwe to use the more expensive South African ports. Zimbabwe reportedly spent around U.S.$3 billion protecting the Beira line between 1980 and 1988. It had to send increasing numbers of troops into Mozambique, and Renamo responded with attacks on civilian targets in Manicaland, claiming numerous civilian lives. On top of such troubles the country also had to host hundreds of thousands of refugees from Mozambique. The Reagan administration and the Thatcher government benignly ignored South Africa's campaign of destabilization (mainly economic) against independent Zimbabwe, which lasted a whole decade.

ZAPU V. ZANU

Internally, old rivalries between ZANU and ZAPU supporters soon resurfaced; these eventually led to open conflict within a year of independence. On the discovery of an arms cache on ZAPU-owned farms in 1982, Nkomo came under suspicion for plotting a coup. His party's assets were seized, ZAPU ministers were dismissed from government, and its key military leaders were arrested. Ndebele soldiers deserted from the Zimbabwe army and resumed guerrilla warfare against the government as dissidents. Mugabe responded by sending the Fifth Brigade into Nkomo's constituency of Matebeleland in 1982. There was a heavy loss of Ndebele life, and Nkomo fled the country for Botswana, where he remained until Mugabe relented and invited him back with a guarantee of his safety; he also offered an amnesty to the dissidents. Thereafter, the two sides entered into discussions and reached an agreement in 1987 to merge ZANU and ZAPU. Another token of reconciliation was the decision to locate Zimbabwe's second university in Bulawayo and to document ZAPU *chimurenga* dead along with ZANU ones. In 1987 the two parties agreed to a Unity Pact, as a result of which they merged, retaining the name of the dominant party, ZANU.

In 1990 the Lancaster House constitution expired on its tenth anniversary, enabling the government to begin a review of the land-owning privileges that it had guaranteed whites, and in 1998 the government did away with the constitutional provision reserving twenty seats to them in parliament.

CORRUPTION AND REPRESSION

Zimbabwe has not been spared the woes that have beset most independent African countries, including official corruption and impatience with opposition. Mugabe's preference was for a one-party constitution, but there was considerable opposition to the idea in the country, even within his own party. In the March 1990 elections, Edgar Tekere's new Zimbabwe Unity Movement (ZUM) challenged ZANU, but its chances of any success were derailed by government electoral tampering. ZANU won in a landslide, its agents harassed ZUM supporters into submission, and Takere was later wounded in an assassination attempt. Nevertheless, the ZANU central committee, fearing adverse international reaction, voted overwhelmingly against a one-party constitution.

With regard to official corruption, the open graft and cupidity of high government officials, including the allocation to themselves of land abandoned by fleeing whites, as well as other forms of embezzlement, caused protests by students angry that Mugabe had failed to keep his promise to run a corruption-free government. Student protests in 1988 provoked Mugabe into shutting down the university until the protesters relented, but the move did not put an end to dissent. In 1997 it came from workers miffed at the ostentatious marriage of Mugabe to Grace Marufu in August of that year, at a time when the country's economy was in shambles and workers could hardly make ends meet. The government's response was un-compromising: it terminated the employment of all strikers.

INTERVENTION IN THE DRC

In 1998 the Mugabe government joined other regional countries in interven-ing in the Democratic Republic of the Congo (DRC) to help Lauren Kabila fight off his enemies. The hugely expensive move has placed a severe strain on the economy, but the most serious problem independent Zimbabwe has had to face, which it has not yet solved, is the unequal distribution of land. Whites made up less than 3 percent of the population (270,000) at indepen-dence, a figure that had declined to less than 1 percent by 1990, but they hold on to a third of the best lands in the country, which cannot be taken from them without their consent and adequate compensation. The funds available to the government for the acquisition of such lands for redistribu-tion to Africans are woefully inadequate, and toward the end of 1990 Mugabe announced his intention, against the advice of white farmers' unions, to seize 50 percent of white-held lands for redistribution to African families. He soon backed down, though, because he had no desire to make any moves that might frighten away either the white farmers (who were responsible for almost half of the country's annual income) or foreign investors. A similar fate awaited the Land Acquisition Act of 1992, which aimed to appropriate 5 million hectares of commercial farmland and redistribute them to 1 million black families for subsistence farming. The problem persists, offering Mugabe a convenient issue to exploit whenever his popularity wanes—appeasing land-deprived Africans, especially war veterans who insist on the takeover of white-owned farms, by force if necessary, for their own benefit. In the run-up to the 1995 elections he used his proclaimed intention to seize land from whites and redistribute it to blacks to shore up his slipping popularity, for neither the first nor the last time. Land was again a major issue in the June 2000 elections, which were preceded by the occupation of white-owned farms by veterans of Zimbabwe's *chimurenga*, with the quite open support of Mugabe. Cynics saw his stance as a gambit to win an election in which the opposition alliance, the Movement for Democratic Change, seemed poised to topple the governing party. In the event Mugabe and his party won, but with only a bare majority.

Deepening Crisis

The success of the MDC in the 2000 elections and Mugabe's plummeting popularity encouraged the hope in some quarters that he would depart the political arena, but he put such hopes to rest with an April 2001 announcement of his intention to be a candidate for the presidency in the 2002 elections. As in the past, he and his party, ZANU-PF have forged a working alliance with the war veterans who have engaged in increasingly violent actions against MDC opponents, white farmers, and even urban factories and businesses. The government's endorsement of farm occupations is evident in the passage of The Rural Land Occupiers (Protection from Eviction) Act, which was signed into law on June 5, 2001. It retroactively gave land invaders and occupiers the ownership of the lands they had alienated before March 1, 2001.[5]

The collapse of law and order in the country prompted Malawi president Bakili Muluzi, the leader of a Southern African Development Conference (SADC) delegation that visited Harare in September 2001, to complain that state-sponsored violence in Zimbabwe was causing economic problems for the whole region.[6] The delegation's visit followed a meeting of Commonwealth foreign ministers in Abuja, Nigeria, which sought to remove the land problem as an issue ZANU-PF and Mugabe could continue to exploit. The U.S. Senate indicated its concern with the passage, on August 2, 2002, of the Zimbabwe Democracy Act, which called for travel and economic sanctions against perpetrators and their families of acts contributing to the breakdown of law and order.[7]

The toll of the crisis, exacerbated by the ruinous intervention in the DRC, is reflected in the collapse of the country's economy: in January 2001 commercial farmers moved to lay off more than 300,000 workers;[8] normally a net exporter of maize, the country must instead import approximately 600,000 tons of the country's staple food this year, due largely to the farm crisis worsened by erratic rainfall;[9] and the inflation rate, officially set at 70 percent, is widely believed to be actually between 300 and 400 percent.[10]

NOTES

1. T. V. Bulpin, quoted in Deanna Swaney, *Zimbabwe, Botswana and Namibia* (Hawthorn, Australia: Lonely Planet Publications, 1999), 18.
2. Peter Garlake, *Great Zimbabwe Described and Explained* (Harare: Zimbabwe Publishing House, 1982).
3. Dickson A. Mungazi, *To Honor the Sacred Trust of Civilization: History, Politics, and Education in Southern Africa* (Cambridge, MA: Schenkman Publishing Co., 1983), 277.
4. Ibid., 281.
5. International Crisis Group Africa Briefing Paper, "Zimbabwe: Time for International Action." October 12, 2001, 10.
6. Ibid, 4.

7. Anna Husarska, "Ground Zimbabwe's Jet-Setting Despots." Comment published in the *Washington Post*, Tuesday August 21, 2001, A17. International Crisis Group on-line system: http://www.crisisweb.org/projects/showreport.cfm?reportid=39.
8. International Crisis Group Africa Report No. 32, "Zimbabwe in Crisis: Finding a Way Forward," July 12, 2001, 6.
9. International Crisis Group Africa Briefing Paper, "Zimbabwe: Time for International Action." October 12, 2001, 11.
10. Ibid.

2

Thought and Religion

RELIGION

CHRISTIANITY IS THE MAIN RELIGION in Zimbabwe, commanding the allegiance of an estimated 40–50 percent of the population. A Portuguese attempt to establish Christianity in the area in 1561 proved abortive, and it was the Reverend Robert Moffat of the London Missionary Society who laid the firm foundation of the religion at Inyati in 1859. African members of the Dutch Reformed Church in South Africa followed soon after, and in 1880 Jesuit missionaries established themselves in Lobengula's kraal. The Methodists and Anglicans came later. The Catholic Church, which was of minor significance until the 1950s, is now larger than any of the Protestant sects—Methodist, Anglican, Salvation Army, Seventh-Day Adventist, Dutch Reformed, Presbyterian, Congregational, Episcopalian, North American Apostolic (fundamentalist and charismatic), and African churches—whose adherents number about a million. The Asian minority adhere mainly to either Islam or Hinduism, and there are Jewish and Greek Orthodox communities in the main urban centers.

The Zimbabwe Assemblies of God, which became independent in 1960, also has a large following, and has expanded to other nearby countries. The Vapostori are an indigenous evangelical sect who, among other things, avoid the use of medicine. These are two of the independent African churches operating in the country. They are Pentecostal in nature, and their worship services often involve spirit possession, speaking in tongues, and revelations, features with which Zimbabweans are familiar in their traditional religious practices, and that make this brand of Christianity seem much less alien.

With the exception of the Jesuits, the early missionary groups in the area started schools and offered social and medical services, and also gave agricultural assistance. In 1972, at the height of the fight to topple the Smith regime, the Catholic Church distinguished itself by establishing the Catholic Commission for Justice and Peace to monitor human rights violations and promote social justice. It continues to work alongside the Catholic Development Commission, which focuses on rural social and economic development.

TRADITIONAL RELIGION AND IDEAS OF GOD

Mwari

Shona religion is monotheistic; the people believe in a Supreme Being who, like the Christian God, created and sustains the universe. They call him Mwari (literally, "He who is").[1] There is a tradition, though, that depicts him not as "the Eternal Causeless Cause,"[2] but as himself created, as the first of all creation.[3] In this tradition Mwari is the original ancestor, the first person created in Guruuswa, believed by the Shona to be the ultimate original site. As a disembodied spirit whose voice comes down from the sky, he led the ancestors of the Shona from Guruuswa to *nyika dzinó* (these lands), the present home of the Shona. Mwari, in this account, is a founding ancestor close to the time of creation, but not the creator. In keeping with his manifestation as a voice, people refer to him as Soko, meaning "Voice" or "Word," one who makes himself heard in the thunder, and whose blessing is often in the form of rain.

Mwari Cult in the Matopos

Historically, the Mwari cult dates to the late seventeenth century; Shona migrants known as the Torwa from the disintegrated Great Zimbabwe settled in the Matopos region and established a dynasty in the fifteenth century with their headquarters at Khami. There they built a centralized state after the pattern of the Great Zimbabwe and ruled until they were displaced in the 1680s by the Rozvi. These were another Shona group, a remnant of the Mutapa state to the north, led by their *mambo* (king), and it was under them that the Mwari cult became established. The king was himself a medium of Mwari, serving as the god's spokesman when he became possessed by the *mhondoro* (tribal spirits; see below).

Mwari did not concern himself with trifles or individuals' affairs, but with matters that affected the well-being of the entire community, especially the provision of good rain. Otherwise the ancestral spirits held sway. At the turn of the nineteenth century, the king, with his seat at Danangombe, became impatient with Mwari's interference in state affairs and chased the spirit off with gunfire. The enraged Mwari in response cursed the community, invoking a plague of "men wearing skins." These turned out to be Nguni raiders, the first of whom came under Zwangendaba. The king fled before them to the Matopos and eventually jumped off a cliff. By the time the next wave of Nguni arrived under Mzilikazi, the Rozvi state was in disarray. Mzilikazi ingratiated himself with the Mwari cult by sending regular offerings to the spirit. Later, white settler-farmers also recognized the expediency of doing the same, in particular as an insurance against drought.

Attributes

There is a Shona belief that Mwari created the world from nothing and brought man out of "a hole or marsh in the ground, or from a tree."[4] Despite the frequent reference to him as Creator, though, his attributes reflect the uncertainty and ambivalence that surround his status. He is "the Great Spirit," who "piles up rocks to make mountains, causes branches to grow and gives rain to mankind."[5] He is Musiki (Creator), Musikavanhu (Origin of Man), Nyadenga (Father of the Skies, or the Great One of the Sky), Wokumusoro (the One Above), and Dzivaguru (Big Pool). There is some dispute about this last, though, some scholars arguing that it refers not to Mwari but, rather, to "a tribal spirit of very great moment among the Makorekore."[6]

A praise song in Mwari's honor refers to him as "ours even since Guruuswa," and continues, "You are the one who began to be, found already there, original pool," testifying to his status at least as the original being, if not the Creator. It also presents Mwari as leader, father, and mother:

> Leader in the way, Mwari of all the people,
> You are our father, you are our mother,
> Whose breast feeds the whole land unto satiety.

It is not insignificant that the foregoing lines combine both male and female attributes in the Mwari figure, a fact that the customary reference to him with masculine pronouns tends to belie. The song goes on to represent Mwari as omnipotent, "Immovable and wondrous as a medicine that feeds upon grass," as well as omnipresent and infinite: "Like a plant that creeps everywhere, where you go we cannot follow; / You encompass the land, girdle without beginning or end."

Mwari is also one who is bounteous as well as merciful,

> Whose blessing fills the forests, gentle rain that falls on all,
> Wind through a cave that makes no noise in passing.
> . . .
>
> Leader in the way, lord never stretching his leg in annoyance.
> Beauty that would elsewhere be omen, never provoking a quarrel.

He is a succorer and provider:

> In trouble, danger, and pain, and in sadness as well
> We remember you both night and day.
> All our woes are your burden.
> It is you who deliver us from our ills.
> You who serve out to us our daily food.
> You who care for us all.

But he also chastises, presumably when he wishes to alert the people to the need to correct some error in their ways. The concluding lines of the song remind one powerfully of some of the songs of penitence in the biblical book of Psalms:

> We weep on your account in these evil times.
> You have brought us into them.
> You then will guard us in all adversities.[7]

Mwari makes his presence felt through earthquakes, which the Shona interpret as the sound of his taking a walk. They also see his manifestation in stars, comets, and meteors, in lightning and storms, and in such awesome phenomena as the Matopo Mountains.

Although the Ndebele join the rest of the country in worshiping Mwari (whom they call uMlimu), they yet maintain belief in their own supreme being, or God, Unkulunkulu. The Zulu name suggests ultimate greatness, and for the Ndebele it means "the Supremely Great One."

Mwari Worship

At the time of the Ndebele invasion Mwari's cult was already the established religion of the Rozvi, and it soon won the allegiance of the conquerors. The cult is secret, and accordingly knowledge of it is confined to initiates. There would appear, though, to be some disagreement about the real identity of the supreme being, inasmuch as he bears different names in different locations in Zimbabwe. The Ndebele know him as uMlimu; Gelfand cautions, though, that "the Mlimo is probably another great tribal spirit corresponding to Chaminuka and Dzivaguru [see below] and controls the rain of south-western parts of Mashonaland."[8] The Kalanga cite him as the spirit which, like other tribal spirits, controls the rain, thunder, lightning, and wind, and whose voice can be heard in the depths of the Matopo caves. The MaKorekore for their part recognize Chikara as the supreme being and creator. But a consideration of the attributes of these figures suggests that the designations Mwari, Chikara, and uMlimu (Mlimo) all belong to the same entity, but in different parts of Zimbabwe, whether in Mashonaland or in Matabeleland.

The Shona do not have myths concerning the origin of the world to go with any belief that Mwari created the universe; what myths they have pertain to the first *mhondoro* or tribal spirits. A Zezuru account states that long ago, before the appearance of the first *mhondoro*, a special tree that grew at a place called Marinjari fell down and shoots sprouted from it. From the log came a voice that the people recognized as that of Mwari. It commanded the people who had assembled to hear it to shut their eyes, and when they later opened them, they beheld a rich feast with abundant beer laid on the ground. After they had eaten and drunk to their satisfaction, the voice asked them again to shut their eyes, and on reopening them they saw that all trace of the feast was gone, but not their feeling of satiety.

To the extent that there is direct worship of Mwari, it takes place in shrines usually located in caves and sacred mountains throughout the country. The most important of these is at Matonjeni under the care of a priest and a priestess. Its influence is such that it extracts tribute from the surrounding Ndebele and even from the nearby white farmers, on account of Mwari's presumed discretion in sending the rain on which so much depends. The white farmers pay the tribute as a form of insurance, just in case there is some validity to the folk belief in Mwari's power with regard to rain-making. At harvest time the Shona themselves offer sacrifices and prayers to Mwari in gratitude for his bounty. The oracle or "voice" here is an elderly woman who speaks an unintelligible language that requires translation for visitors' benefit. There are other active shrines near Bulawayo, at Njelele and Wirarani in the Matopo Hills, and at Dula near Esigodini.

Being a sky god, Chikara (or Mwari, or uMlimu) is indifferent to human affairs. He has so far removed himself from the earth that he is inaccessible to humans, but he long ago delegated great spirits (*mhondoro*) to provide the people with abundant rainfall and bountiful crops. The *mhondoro* are less powerful than Mwari but quite active in all human affairs. Beneath them in hierarchy are the spirits of ancestors, *midzimu*, also *vadzimu* (*mudzimu* in the singular), the Ndebele equivalent being *amadhlozi*.

The Mambo (King)

Traditionally, the king (*mambo*) was regarded as a god, and his authority came directly from Mwari. He lived lavishly with his wives, concubines, and officials, and when he held public audiences, he was concealed from public gaze by a screen. Supplicants approached him creeping and clapping to show homage. On his death his queens and some ministers were buried with him, and all the fires in the land were extinguished, since the king was the giver of fire. The fires would be rekindled at the accession of the new king.[9] Yet the king's authority was severely limited. He had to be flawless, and if he became seriously ill he had to commit suicide. He lived isolated from the people, and was therefore dependent on his officials, courtiers, and queens, who in fact exercised much of his power. The authority of the king therefore depended a great deal on the force of his personality.

As with other African peoples, Shona kingship was divine, and like other kings the Shona *mambo* kept the sons of vassal kings at court, ostensibly to train them, but in reality to keep their fathers on their best behavior. The Rowzi king often served as a *svikiro* (spirit medium; see below). The Great Zimbabwe testifies to the power of the king and the people's regard for him; indeed, the complex is believed to have been designed to demonstrate just those points. It is also significant that he and his counselors lived within the enclosure, while the general population lived outside the walls.

Mhondoro

The word *mhondoro* means "lion" in Shona; it attests to the leonine ferociousness of these tribal or tutelary spirits. Each clan has its own *mhondoro*, which is the spirit of the ancestral founder of that clan, and whose actions affect whole peoples and communities. It protects the community when pleased, giving it plentiful rainfall, for example, and causing such afflictions as droughts, epidemic diseases, and such like when displeased. The recognized "national spirits," "super-*mhondoro*," or great spirits (*midzimu mikurukuru*), are Mambiri, Tovera, Murenga, Runni, Chaminuka, Mushavatu, and Nehanda.[10] There is a hierarchy among these spirits; in certain parts of the country Chaminuka and Dzivaguru are the most important, the first operating among the Central Mashona (MaZezuru), while the second belongs to the MaKorekore. Chaminuka appears to be the greater of the two, being recognized as the Tateguru (Great Father), the spirit of the original, common ancestor. The people believe that the voice from the log at Marinjari belonged to the spirit Chaminuka before it possessed its first medium. In general, though, *mhondoro* are not localized in any areas, for all the Shona people claim them.

The head *mhondoro* of each region is considered next to God the Creator (Chikara). Dzivaguru was the first on the scene before the others arrived, and he was next to Chikara. He departed (or disappeared) when the others arrived, but he is still consulted in extremities. Dzivaguru would then correspond to Chaminuka, whom the MaZezuru hold to be above all tribal spirits. Nonetheless, other groups hold that their own tribal spirits (Nehanda for example) are able to communicate directly with Chikara without going through Chaminuka. The spirits of dead kings are also considered to be intermediaries between God and the people.

Most abhorrent to the *mhondoro* are the crimes of incest and murder, for which the whole group may be punished with drought, pestilence, or visitation by wild animals. People pray to them for rain before planting seeds, or at the sampling of seeds as they ripen in the field, or in propitiation to stave off their anger after a clan member has committed a crime. Such ceremonies are usually the responsibility of the chief, who provides the ingredients and the beer brewed for the purpose.

Vadzimu

The primary contacts for humans in the spirit world are the *vadzimu* (Shona), or *amadhlozi* (Ndebele). These are "spirit elders," the spirits of the departed members of the family unit, who are present within the living community, caring for their descendants and sharing their experiences, although they remain invisible. Along with *mhondoro*, they are the spirits that possess mediums, and to whom the Mashona turn for help in times of difficulty. They differ from the *mhondoro* in that they are identified with particular families rather than the whole clan. A *mudzimu* is the spirit of a person's father or grandfather, the most important being the spirit of the father or grandfather of the oldest family member. *Vadzimu* (or *mudzimu*) (pl.) are the spirits to which members of a family turn, because they are primarily interested in their own children. In each home is a shrine to the *mudzimu*; he receives special home-brewed millet beer at an annual ceremony, and is consulted on other occasions. *Mudzimu* impose restrictions on their descendants, like forbidding the use of certain "modern" materials, as each tries to enforce behavior current in its lifetime. They pay close attention to the affairs of the living, communicate with them through mediums, protect those who deserve protection, and visit those who so deserve with misfortune. A person so afflicted consults a medium to determine which ancestor is displeased with him/her. The family gathers in a *bira* (a spirit possession session during which people communicate with ancestors through mediums) during which the *mudzimu* is invoked; it possesses the victim and states its grievance as well as what will appease it. Afterwards the person concerned becomes the family medium of that particular ancestor spirit.

The restrictions the *mhondoro* and the *midzimu* impose on the living generation have been variously interpreted as inhibiting and beneficial. In one view,

> [t]he qualities favoured by these spirits are good behaviour, respect for elders, and conformity to the life led by one's fathers, seeking little or no wealth or position. It follows that material progress, especially material progress of an individual, is unlikely to result in this traditional society. We know that there has been little change in the mode of life over generations and that any influence liable to break up the family has been opposed.[11]

But according to another, the goal of their sanctions is to maintain justice, social order, and group cohesiveness. "Families can demand compensation for wrongs committed long ago to an ancestor by another family; the descendants of people who failed to stop someone being killed in their village are considered guilty of a crime against the ancestors, and a man who insults his mother will face continual bad luck, even after her death, until he puts things right. You ignore the ancestral spirits . . . at your peril, whatever the missionaries might tell you on Sundays about worshiping idols."[12]

Svikiro

Mhondoro and *vadzimu* communicate with humans through mediums (*svikiro*) whom they choose at random, through dream revelation, for example. The medium of a *mhondoro* assumes leonine characteristics, growling its messages, which require interpretation by an acolyte (*nechombo*). Mediums are subject to some taboos. Typically, the medium must avoid certain things of European origin, such as cigarettes, tea, and sugar, although he may use snuff. He may not receive medical attention from a European doctor or an African doctor who practices Western medicine, nor may he enter a hospital; he may be treated only by a *n'anga* (traditional healer; see below). He may not wash with soap, other than a locally made type, and he may not wear shoes or boots, but a flat sandal which exposes the toes, and whose sole is made of rubber, leather, or cloth. Other prohibitions have nothing to do with Western connections; they include such things as avoidance of foods like tomatoes, onions, chicken, buffalo or hippopotamus meat, guinea-fowl, or zebra. Finally, mediums may not use charms or make incisions on their bodies. Some mediums cook their own food in their own huts, rather than letting their wives cook for them.

For the most part, apart from when they are performing their ritual duties, mediums live like ordinary people, working their farms and tending their cattle. But they typically wear their distinctive white attire, which consists of a loincloth and a shawl, both made from white sheeting. The loincloth is wrapped around the waist, with one end passed between the legs from front to back, and tucked in at the back of the waist. The shawl is thrown over the shoulders. One of the essential props for a medium (especially during possession) is a ceremonial wooden staff about four feet long and one inch in diameter, decorated along almost its entire length with finely woven copper wire.

A medium can sometimes exert powerful influence on the people, as did Nehanda during the first *chimurenga*. She was possessed by the spirit of one of the most powerful *mhondoro*, Mbuya Nehanda, Chaminuka's sister, whose mediums are always respected women with exceptional leadership abilities, and who, once chosen for their new role, must remain single and adopt the name Mbuya Nehanda. At the time of the conflict with the white settlers in 1896, the medium was a woman named Nyakasikana; working in concert with Gumboreshumba, who was himself possessed by the spirit of Sekuru Kaguvi, she incited the people to rise up in opposition to settlers. It is a mark of their influence and effectiveness that they were hanged for their activities.

Another tradition about Nehanda (the *mhondoro*) is that she died while leading her people to cross the Zambezi to their new home; her death came before she accomplished the goal, but her spirit went into a medium, who pointed a wooden rod at the river, thus parting the waters and allowing the people to cross. The unmistakable similarity to the service Moses rendered to the wandering Israelites leads to the suggestion that this tradition most probably bears the stamp of Christian missionary influence.

N'anga

These are traditional healers who derive their power from *midzimu* and *shave* (vengeful spirits). They are evidence of the ancestors' active involvement in ministrations to the sick. *N'anga* (*nganga*) are able to consult the spirits through the use of divining dice, the Shona wooden bones, animal bones, or *mungomo* (seeds popular among the Ndebele), and are versed in the knowledge of medicinal herbs, their efficacious applications and limitations. They also exorcise evil spirits, sending them into animals or imprisoning them in stoppered bottles, which are then abandoned in the bush, where the trapped spirits await any hapless person who finds them and releases them from their prison. Although in general they combine preventive, curative, and divinatory functions, a specialization does exist in their ranks, according to which the *chiremba* (pl. *zviremba*) are only herbal doctors who do not engage in divining like other *n'anga*.

The *n'anga* is, in effect, the priest of the family. In the past he possessed the gift of finding food or of hunting. These days some have the gift of understanding and behaving like Europeans, a useful asset in the modern atmosphere.

An illness could result from one's breaching a taboo or neglecting a necessary ritual, and it could be a delayed repercussion for the unexpiated misdeeds of long-dead ancestors. The cure requires that a *n'anga* perform the required treatment, and in the case of an attack by a witch or wizard (see below), identify and punish the miscreant.

Shave (Vengeful Spirits)

Unlike *midzimu*, who can be beneficial or malevolent, *shave* are the vengeful spirits of dead strangers who were killed unjustly or denied proper burial. The significance of the cult, which is believed to be inherited from men of foreign origin who died in Mashonaland, is not clear, apart from the fact that it provides an avenue for an aspirant to become a *n'anga*. The malevolent spirit enters only selected people, and a close relation of the medium offers prayers to it on special occasions. The manifestation of its visitation is usually a chronic illness or erratic behavior suggesting mental derangement. To be cured the victim must be initiated as a *n'anga*. The vengeful spirits confer talents on their mediums, including the ability to treat diseases and the gift of divination.

Witches

The Shona, in common with many African peoples, seldom attribute illnesses to such mundane causes as environmental contamination or physiological disorders, preferring malevolent agencies instead. The same goes for many deaths, especially sudden ones or those of young people. Witches are frequent suspects, and so are vengeful spirits and evil spirits. Accusations of witchcraft often result from jealousy or resentment of the accused person for any reason. There are two kinds of witches: those who acquired the trait, and those who inherited it; but in either case they are believed to send malevolent, diminutive spirits to attack people who ostentatiously display their wealth or hoard it, especially wealth in the form of imported luxury goods, fancy clothing, skin cream, automobiles, and the like. They also attack rich people who have not been generous to their kin.

Ndebele medicine men perform functions similar to those of their Shona counterparts: they combat witchcraft and magic, prevent their action, and sometimes send them back to their authors. In addition they supply medicated pegs for the gates of new homesteads, and they perform the ceremony of "striking the grave" when a person dies of witchcraft. The ceremony takes place at sunset in the presence of the son and brother of the deceased. The medicine man strikes the grave with his medicine stick, saying, "So-and-so, wake up! Go and fight!" The spirit of the deceased is then supposed to arise and go in the form of an animal to the witch's house. There it remains until a member of the family sees and kills the animal. Thereupon the members of the household begin to die off. If the rest admit guilt, they pay cattle to the family of the deceased, and a powerful medicine man is employed to lift the curse from them.

The *n'anga*, being the ones who, through dreams, detect who is a witch or wizard and how to treat the effects of witchcraft, are in reality responsible for the existence of witchcraft, or at least they sustain the belief in the phenomenon.

Ngozi

Ngozi are the restless and vengeful spirits of people who died aggrieved. Four types of *ngozi* have been identified: the spirit of a murdered person; the spirit of a servant who was not paid for his services, or of someone from whom something was taken or borrowed and not returned; the spirit of a husband or wife who died unhappy by the spouse's treatment of him or her; and the spirit of a parent wronged by his/her child. A *ngozi* makes its presence known by possessing a person, usually someone from the family of the offender, and uses that person as a medium.

A *n'anga* may specialize in recognizing *ngozi* possession and dealing with them, usually by arranging a *bira* (see below). Once the offender has paid the required reparation, no further problem arises. As an instance of how a *ngozi* operates, a woman, Maria, was possessed by a *ngozi*, which revealed itself as that of one Chiutzi. He had been wrongfully denounced by villagers during the second *chimurenga* as committing adultery with the wife of an absent freedom fighter, and had been killed by other fighters. At the *bira* arranged on the occasion, Chiutzi demanded that Maria become his wife, and she did: she was sent to become a member of Chiutzi's family.[13]

Bira

A Shona observer describes the *bira* as the most important event in the social calendar of the village, with the possible exception of funerals. The *bira* is an important institution among the Shona, for it is the most elaborate means of communication between the living and the living dead. The object of the *bira* is possession, which is also the most distinctive aspect of Shona religion. It is induced by suitable music, usually the spirited playing of a mbira ensemble, but on some occasions the mere clapping of hands by an assistant to the medium is enough to induce the state. It is customarily an all-night ceremony during which family members assemble to seek help from a common ancestor through a medium. Furthermore, if a *n'anga* determines that a person's problem results from the desire of a spirit to possess the victim, for whatever reason, he advises the family to arrange for a *bira*.

The family staging the *bira* brews special ritual beer for the occasion in honor of the ancestors, and usually hires a mbira ensemble to provide the music. The ceremony starts at sundown, with the immediate family and neighbors present. They shed their shoes and watches, because the spirits are put off by the sight of objects that they were not familiar with when they were human beings. The men sit segregated from the women and the children, and the people drink beer from specially designated pots (each category of people, mediums, for example, having its separate pot). The mediums sit on mats facing the musicians, and listen to the problems that have caused the family to arrange the *bira*. Such occasions are also opportunities for identifying mediums, as potential ones distinguish themselves by unusual behavior, and the calling is usually confirmed at a *bira* ceremony. Once identified as such, each medium becomes the exclusive "mount" of one spirit, which can be induced to possess its medium by certain known songs. In the state of possession the medium assumes the personality of his particular spirit, and enjoys considerable regard in that role.

Biras were usually held on the land occupied by the ancestors, but white evictions have made these difficult in recent years. Now they take place in specially built enclosures used only on religious occasions, or in a village round house converted for the occasion. The tradition makes it possible for the living to remain in continual contact with their ancestors. Since people cannot approach Mwari directly, only through ancestors, the *bira* enables them to ask the latter for intercession with the deity. It also often serves as a means of enforcing the moral values of the society, as, for instance, when a medium revealed that a child's illness was brought about by ancestors' anger that the child's grandfather had held on to the property that rightfully belonged to his deceased wife, instead of returning it to her family, as custom dictated. In another, less salutary instance, an innocent man was proclaimed a wicked person during a *bira*, simply because the people were jealous of the flashy lifestyle of his wife, a local woman who had returned from the city with him; the couple had to leave the village and return to the city. The *bira* also proved its efficacy in political organization: in the 1970s mediums went from place to place, delivering messages during *bira*s that had hidden political meanings.

AMALGAMATIONS OF BELIEFS

Although Christianity and traditional religions are theoretically distinct and separate, in practice there is a significant degree of mixture of the two: traditional beliefs and practices meet and mix with Christian ones. People profess Christianity without abandoning the traditional spirits or turning their backs on observances designed to honor the ancestors, ensure their pleasure, and ascertain their wishes. Among both the Shona and the Ndebele, the adoption of Christianity was often a calculated and expedient decision. In the early days doing so was the only certain means of gaining access to the services and amenities the missions provided, health care, for example. Moreover, because the religion was associated with the dominant white settlers, inasmuch as the Western way came to be regarded as the way of the future, it inevitably came to be invested with prestige and progressiveness: to be a Christian was to be better, socially and often materially, than the unconverted. Furthermore, the church congregation and its clubs provided urban dwellers with a substitute for the social infrastructure they left behind when they moved away from their villages. For these reasons, the profession of Christianity did not, and does not, necessarily preclude continued belief in Mwari or participation in traditional religious rituals. A commentator observes, "It is not unusual to hear African Christians refer to Jesus as universal *mudzimu*. As *Mudzimu Mukuru* (the great ancestral spirit). He becomes incarnated within African culture and in that way people can understand His role and participation in all aspects of life, rather than being confined to ecclesiastical or to spiritual matters."[14]

One source of friction between Christians and adherents of traditional religious practices revolves around the issue of witchcraft. The 1890 Witchcraft Suppression Act specifies punishment for practicing witchcraft, accusing people of witchcraft, and witch-hunting. Since 1997 the Zimbabwe National African Traditional Healers' Association has been trying to get the act amended to redefine witchcraft such that it applies only to intents to cause illness, injury, or death. But the Christian churches and civil rights groups have opposed such a move, because they argue that the law as it stands protects people falsely accused of witchcraft, especially women.

Belief and Personal Hygiene

Many of the practices involving personal hygiene and related matters bespeak fear of witches. People were concerned to keep bodily waste off the hands of potential witches. Magic was also implicated in much cosmetic "smearing":

> The *muti* [medicine] of the *n'anga* [herbalist] included many pastes, unguents, and cleansers to purify, heal, and protect clients. . . . Among the Ndebele . . . those who remained behind when an *impi* [battle regiment] was dispatched into battle were supposed to refrain from washing until the regiment returned. Likewise, in a few Shona-speaking areas, the relatives of a dead person did not wash until the body was safely buried. Among Shona speakers, the corpse was (and still often is) washed carefully by *vasahwira* [close friends or occasionally senior relatives with ritual responsibilities]; after the funeral, *vasahwira* and other mourners were careful to wash themselves thoroughly. In some villages, at the *nhaka* [inheritance] ceremony sometime after a death, the son of the deceased was ritually washed by the *dunzvi* [a senior paternal relative who led the ceremony].[15]

The Significance of the Land

The abode of the ancestors is Pasí (the ground, or the world below). The ancestors who inhabit Pasí are the ones the living generation still remembers, and whom the people still invoke and consult. The importance of the land derives from the fact of the ancestors' burial in it, and their having passed it on to the present generation. The people's close connection with the land, and thus with the ancestors, finds expression in the practice of referring to a person who lives on ancestral land as a child of the soil, a designation that sets him or her apart from a sojourner who lacks the psychic connection.

According to a Shona tale, Mwari apportioned goods to certain men such that one man received people, another cattle, and a third a handful of soil. The man who received the soil was by that token entitled to claim ownership of all that grew in or fell on the soil, people and cattle included.

Traditionally, no individual owned land, all land being the chief's property, and the chief holding it in trust on behalf of the whole community as their direct link with the ancestors. Indeed, the land belongs to the spirits of the ancestors, and the tradition of *chisi*, the dedication of sacred days to ancestral spirits during which no work may be done on the soil, persists. The psychic or mystical importance of the land explains the practice of holding the *bira* on ancestral land, and the substitution of other venues is an expedient imposed by circumstances.

The Importance of Water

"Water is associated with life. . . . Water purifies, restores, cleanses and re-generates."[16] We have already noted the importance the people attach to good rainfall, and the consequent need to avoid offending Mwari and the tribal spirits. To the Shona, pools are sacred abodes of spirits and deities, as places to go to when prayers are necessary to end droughts. Water also features prominently in the calling of *n'anga*; people sometimes disappear suddenly only to materialize later dressed as *n'anga*, claiming to have returned from the bottom of a pool where they were taught the mysteries regarding healing and divining by mermaids or ancestral spirits. The medium Chihata claims that at a young age she began to dream repeatedly of flying and falling into the river, and that through dreams she also acquired the power to heal. Diviners whom her parents consulted revealed that she was destined to be a medium, but she resisted the calling, until the spirits dragged her to the bottom of the Magaba River, where they kept her for four days. For the four days her parents and diviners frantically performed certain rituals, and on the fourth day a diviner found her on a rock in the river, wearing a cowrie-shell headband, with a *gano* (ceremonial axe) and a small white ornament beside her. She vomited fish and did not eat for two days. After a *bira* was performed, she embarked on a career as the "important herbalist."[17]

Finally, the Shona bury dead babies in wet soil near the bank of a river, the probable reason being the belief that water will regenerate the young soul, just as it makes seeds grow, and restore it to another family.

Color Symbology

The color black is of major spiritual significance among the Shona, being favored for ritual occasions, along with white and dark blue. At *bira* ceremonies, the medium dons black apparel when he enters into his trance state. Sometimes, a medium may be wearing regular clothes at the beginning of a *bira*, but on becoming possessed will leave the gathering, go home, and return in the proper possession attire. Only then does he become the spirit that has possessed him. Otherwise, the medium's acolyte might be the one to go fetch the correct clothing and dress the medium in it.

Because red is associated with medium possessions, no ordinary person would dance wearing red, for fear of running afoul of the ancestors.

NOTES

1. A. Moyo, "Religion and Political Thought in Independent Zimbabwe," in C. Hallencreutz and A. Moyo, *Church and State in Zimbabwe* (Gweru, Zimbabwe: Mambo Press, 1988), 199.

2. Charles Bullock, *The Mashona (The Indigenous Natives of S. Rhodesia)* (1928; reprint, Westport, CT: Negro Universities Press, 1970), 116.

3. A. C. Hodza and G. Fortune, comps. and eds., *Shona Praise Poetry* (Oxford: Oxford University Press, 1979), 10.

4. John S. Mbiti, *African Religions and Philosophy* (New York: Praeger, 1969), 93–94.

5. Ibid., 35.

6. Michael Gelfand, *Shona Religion, with Special Reference to the Makorekore* (Cape Town, Wynberg, and Johannesburg: Juta & Co., 1962), 141.

7. Hodza and Fortune, 11–12.

8. Gelfand, 141–42.

9. Samkange, *African Saga: A Brief Introduction to African History* (Nashville, TN: Abingdon Press, 1971), 175.

10. Kariamu Welsh-Asante, *Zimbabwe Dance: Rhythmic Forces, Ancestral Voices. An Aesthetic Analysis* (Trenton, NJ: Africa World Press, 2000), 20.

11. Gelfand, 175.

12. Sekai Nzenza-Shand, *Songs to an African Sunset: A Zimbabwean Story* (Melbourne: Lonely Planet Publications, 1997), 32.

13. Ibid., 49–61.

14. Moyo, 202.

15. Timothy Burke, *Lifebuoy Men, Lux Women: Commodification, Consumption, and Cleanliness in Modern Zimbabwe* (Durham, NC: Duke University Press, 1996), 30.

16. Gelfand, 146.

17. Pamela Reynolds, *Traditional Healers and Childhood in Zimbabwe* (Athens: Ohio University Press, 1996), 117–18.

3

Literature and Media

BOTH SHONA AND NDEBELE TRADITIONAL CULTURES are rich in traditional texts, which comprise brief formulations like proverbs, verse forms like praise (panegyric), funerary (elegiac), and love poems, and prose texts like folktales. With the proverbs they reminded one another of the insights that the group had garnered through its collective long experience; with the poems they eulogized their chiefs, the dead, the clan, and loved ones; and with the folktales they entertained themselves and taught some valuable lessons in the process. In addition to these, work songs lightened their chores, and satirical songs poked fun at people whose ways needed correcting. When the new tradition of written literature developed early in the twentieth century, therefore, it was founded on a well-developed tradition, and continues to reflect its influence, especially since the tradition continues to thrive in the villages.

The new art forms have certainly achieved maturity: in recent years, Zimbabwe novelists, poets, and playwrights, and lately filmmakers, have produced some impressive works and won international recognition by winning prestigious awards.

TRADITIONAL LITERATURE

Traditional verbal creativity, which scholars refer to variously as folklore, oral literature, orature, or verbal art, takes the form of short, compact texts like proverbs, or longer prose ones like folktales, and verse compositions like panegyrics or praise poetry. The proverb is perhaps the most familiar of all, because it pervades all forms of verbal expression, whether it be ordinary conversation, folk singing, storytelling, adjudication of disputes, or the composition and performance of praises. Poetic forms are usually associated with formal occasions, a chief's state audience, a clan gathering in the *dare* (meeting place) for a funeral, and such like. Less formal are the poems adults use to entertain themselves (*ndyaringo* or *ndyanguro*).[1] Folktales (*ngano*) are usually told in leisure times, for example in the evenings after the day's work is over and the people have eaten their evening meal. Storytelling entertains, instructs, and fills the space before bedtime.

Proverbs

These are characteristically oblique statements that deliver their meaning in a metaphoric manner, requiring the hearer to do some mental deciphering in order to receive their message. For example, the proverb "A river is filled by its tributaries" may not say much more to a person with limited wit or imagination than the obvious factual statement, but the thoughtful person will (taking the context into account) understand it to say that one cannot discount little things (tributaries), for without them one cannot build up significant assets (the river). Similarly, "A dog returns to where it has been fed" refers to behavior other than a dog's; it says, for example, that if a merchant wants return business, he must always do right by his customers. Finally, "One thumb will not kill a louse" expresses the view that a loner cannot accomplish much; one needs to work with others. The proverb is based on the practice of crushing lice to death between the nails of the two thumbs. One thumb alone would be useless for the task.

Lyric Poetry: Panegyric

This class of poems includes praise and love poetry. Hodza and Fortune divide praises into three types. The first type includes clan praises (*nhéntémbo dzorúdzi*) which might extol the irresistible sexiness and hunting prowess of male clan members, or the chasteness and wifely potential of the women. The second comprises personal praises, for example, praises of wives and lovers (*nhétémbúrirwá dzemúcherecheré*), and those in honor of chiefs, noble warriors, or other personalities of high esteem, and people who have performed commendable services (*kutunha*). Making up the third type are boasts (*madúnhúrirwá ókuzvídumbidzá*).[2] The most formal are the praise poems of rulers and religious figures, while clan praises are less formal.

Praise poetry, like other poetic forms, is usually a spontaneous verses-and-chorus composition "sung" or declaimed by a bard to the accompaniment of the mbira and other instruments. Among the Shona, bards (*marombe*) attended the king when he was at his residence and when he ventured outside or abroad, and loudly sang his praises to the accompaniment of mbira and *dende* (one-stringed guitar). For example, on a chief's approach to a village under his jurisdiction, the village people greeted him with whistling, shrill cries and warriors' warlike feints with their weapons, and general dancing to drumbeats. The women of the village fell to their knees before the chief and "walked" backwards with their fingers sweeping the chief's path, while praise singers performed *kufárírá mámbo* (rejoicing over the chief), singing praises in his honor.[3] The description is typical of what occurred during the time of the Rozvi kings.

The following lines are from a representative panegyric, the praise of a Matumba chief known as Kakunguwo (Little Crow):

> One who yearns to give.
> Small and brave antelope,
> One that sleeps in the sun.
> Son of your mother, Kurehwa.
> "What I have spoken, I have spoken,
> What I have resolved on is final."
> Small spitting lizard.
> Black mamba.
> One who kills for destruction.
> A log swarming with ants,
> Without any place whereby to turn it around.[4]

The poem illustrates the typical construction of the genre, which is to compile the attributes of the subject, enumerating his accomplishments and noteworthy characteristics. In this case, the chief is generous ("yearns to give"), he is constant and resolute, never wavering once he has decided an issue, and both dangerous to confront, like the mamba, and invulnerable, like the log which a host of swarming ants cannot move.

Praises for ordinary people may be informal compositions by such relatives as the sister's son and by privileged friends. And from their adolescent years, young boys learn to compose poems in praise of their girlfriends and to boast of their combat capabilities, while beer often induces older men to vie with one another in singing the attributes of their wives and mothers-in-law in light-hearted, humorous compositions. Other forms of lyric poetry concern themselves with daily activities: work songs accompany pounding grain and weeding the fields, lullabies soothe babies being coddled, other songs are for dancing at parties, and so forth.[5] Women may not be physically present in the meeting place, but often their insulting songs, which they sing in the fields, are audible there, and the targets could be mothers-in-law or suspected witches.

Folktales

The main prose form is the folktale (*ngano*), which usually takes place as a form of entertainment in the evenings, between dinner and bedtime. A persistent misconception is that it is either an activity that adult storytellers engage in for the benefit of children, as a sort of traditional equivalent of formal schooling, or one peculiar to children (in which children tell tales among themselves). For example, *ndyaringo* or *ndyanguro* have been described as "adult entertainment recitals, analogous in their function to the ngano of childhood."[6] In fact, adults participate in storytelling more than children do, and they do so to entertain themselves, even though children are often welcome. An attentive look at any folktale will reveal, moreover, that it was not created by a childish (or childlike) intellect but by a mature, sophisticated, and discerning one.

Stories often include songs that sometimes involve audience participation, songs that advance the plot or simply serve as interludes. The Shona believe that these stories were invented by an ancient storyteller, Sárúngáno, from whom they have passed through succeeding generations to the present day. It is from him that modern storytellers have inherited their title, as indicated in the formula with which they conclude their tales, "*Ndípo pakáperera sárúngáno,*" meaning "That is where the storyteller ended."[7]

The following is an example of a Shona fokltale.

Once upon a time a man went to the bush to dig a game pit trap. He dug and dug until the hole was deep enough to conceal him, and yet he dug. It happened that as he was thus engaged, a lion was on the prowl, hunting for food. It came to the pit in which the man was still digging, and peering over the rim, saw a potential prey. He sat at the edge of the pit, unseen by the digger, and waited.

In the meantime the man's wife came with food for her husband, and while still some distance from the pit she saw the lion peering into the pit. From the dirt flying out of the hole the woman could tell that her husband was in there digging, and that he was in danger of becoming a meal for the lion. Stealthily, she placed her burden of food on the ground and snuck up on the lion from its blind side. When she got to where the animal lay she pounced on its tail and held on. The surprised lion scrambled up and tried to free its tail, and deal mercilessly with the impudent creature who had dared thus to affront him, but despite its wild circling the woman held on, screaming: "Husband, husband, a lion is after you! Come out and kill it with your assegai (spear)! Don't be afraid, for I have it by the tail!"

Hearing the alarm, the husband scrambled out of the pit, and when he saw the raging lion furiously trying to free himself from the woman, he grabbed his assegai and other tools, and putting what he thought was discretion before valor, fled to the safety of his hut.

Three days later, some hunters passed by the scene and saw the spectacle of a woman, obviously fatigued, but desperately holding on to the tail of a lion, who was himself shuffling slowly around in a circle, as if in a daze. The hunters had little difficulty dispatching the lion and saving the woman, whom they escorted to her village. There she confronted her shamefaced husband and told him she would have nothing to do with him any longer. Instead, she went home with one of the brave hunters.

Every tale has a moral. In this particular case, although it might appear that a gender-based criticism is involved, which explodes the myth that the man is always braver than the woman, in fact the lesson is about living up to one's responsibilities. A person who fails in that regard deserves no respect or benefits. Traditional African societies were (and are) free of the so-called battle of the sexes that often sets men and women at loggerheads in the modern context.

MODERN LITERATURE

The profound involvement of Christian missions in Zimbabwean social and cultural transformation is evident in the development of the country's literature. The missions introduced literacy and established the first schools, which educated, cultivated, and encouraged the earliest writers. Attesting further to their instrumentality in propagating the art is the number of publishing outlets they established, providing invaluable opportunities for aspiring authors. These include Mambo Press, Morgenster, Chishawasha Mission, Word of Life Publications, Rhodesia Mission Press, and Daystar.[8]

The colonial administration established the Rhodesia Literature Bureau in 1954 with the aim of encouraging commercial publishers to make literary materials available to African readers. As one of its strategies to develop manuscripts, the bureau sponsored literary competitions that produced several publishable materials. It shaped what authors wrote through writers' workshops, pamphlets, and advice to them, and also vetted all materials intended for publication. Typically, it encouraged and published only African writing that either supported the ideology of the white minority administration or at least posed no challenge to it. The novels published under its auspices, usually in association with religious and commercial publishers, confined themselves to inoffensive social and religious themes. In the circumstances, few Africans took advantage of the limited opportunities to publish, and on the whole white writers like Cynthia Stockley, Gertrude Page, Arthur Cripps, and Doris Lessing dominated the literary scene prior to independence.

The first book published under the bureau's sponsorship was Solomon Mutswairo's *Feso* (1956), named for the hero of the fiction. He is the ambassador whom the good Zezuru chief Nyangombe sent to the court of his tyrannical Nyai counterpart, Chief Pfumojena, to ask for the hand of Chipochedenga (Pfumojena's daughter) in marriage. After some negotiation Feso abducts the willing Chipochedenga and takes her home to his chief. A war ensues between the two chiefs, resulting in the death of the tyrant. Since *Feso* was a Shona novel, the bureau thought it expedient at this pioneering stage to accompany it with the Ndebele piece *Umthawakazi* (1957) by P. S. Mahlangu, a history of the Ndebele that goes back to the first arrival of the Zulu from the north, but concentrates on the history of the Ndebele under Mzilikazi.

Another author whose themes illustrate the bureau's preferences was Patrick F. Chakaipa, a representative example of his writing being *Rudo Ibofu* (Love Is Blind; 1961). The work is about Zingizi's love for Rowesai, and her eventual choice of the love of God over the love of man. Although Rowesai's father had savagely beaten her, almost killing her, when she first decided to become a nun (becasue Zingizi lacked the means to marry her immediately), and although she eventually agreed to escape from her convent and elope with Zingizi, the author contrives to remove her from the scene long enough to be presumed dead and for Zingizi to be betrothed to her sister. When she unexpectedly shows up at the wedding ceremony, back from the dead as it were, and in a nun's habit, there is general rejoicing; even the father is so happy that he converts to Christianity. In a similar vein, other works the bureau and the missions sponsored in the years leading up to the *chimurenga* in various ways aspersed traditional life and institutions and valorized Christianity and the Western way, although some also concerned themselves with the difficulties Africans faced in attempting to reconcile their old ways with the new dispensation.

The first overtly political work was Stanlake Samkange's *On Trial for My Country* (1966), published while the author was studying in the United States. Its subject is Lobengula's doomed efforts to outwit Cecil Rhodes and his collaborators in their scheme to rob him and his people of their land. Charles Mungoshi, another early writer, was already famous for his

Shona-language novel *Makunun'unu maodzamwoyo* (Brooding Breeds Despair; 1970) when in 1972 he published his collection of short stories in English, *Coming of the Dry Season,* about the progressive alienation of young black Rhodesians in the new society. Although the work was not a direct criticism of the white regime, the Smith government nevertheless banned it in 1974, claiming that one of the stories, "The Accident," was subversive, and the book remained banned until 1978.

Waiting for the Rain (1974) is another dramatization of the way in which European influences have radically changed African lives and institutions. In sum, it revolves around the question of succession to the headship of the Mandengu extended family. Tongoona has two sons, Garabha, the elder, and Lucifer, the younger. Because the younger son has a Western education, Tongoona wants him to supplant Garabha as the successor to the headship. For a while Tongoona's own father, Sekuru Mandengu (Old Man), opposes the decision, but he eventually gives in too, symbolically demonstrating how traditional arrangements fall before the westernizing onslaught. Significantly, the debate takes place on the eve of Lucifer's departure on a scholarship to study in Europe.

Wilson Katiyo's fiction reflects his political awareness and activism. His two novels *A Son of the Soil* (1976) and *Going to Heaven* (1979) tell the story of Alexio and the effects of the white presence on his life. The first novel is a poorly developed account of his birth and early life until as a young man he joins other youths in the mountains to fight against white oppression and harassment. The second is about his experiences in exile in England. The works are to some extent autobiographical, for, like the hero of his novels, Katiyo himself got into trouble with the Special Branch (the security police) in Rhodesia and fled to Zambia in 1965, from where he went on to England.

Other writers worked and published in exile, prominent among them being Dambudzo Marechera (1952–1987), whose more or less autobiographical works deal with the plight of the common people. His childhood was troubled and full of privations, but his intellectual brilliance won him valuable educational opportunities, including a scholarship to Oxford University after he was expelled from the University of Rhodesia in 1973 for antigovernment activities. But his erratic and ungovernable behavior forced him out of Oxford after only two years. During his short career he published some brilliant works, including poetry, fiction, and drama, but at his death he left several complete works unpublished, mainly because he had managed to antagonize his publishers and promoters. His publications include *The House of Hunger* (1978), *Black Sunlight* (1980), *Mindblast, or the Definitive Buddy* (1984), *The Black Insider* (1990), *Cemetery of the Mind: Collected Poems of Dambudzo Marechera* (1992), and *Scrapiron Blues* (1994).

Post-Independence Novels

In the aftermath of independence, writing turned to the exploration of difficult post-independence experiences, with the emergence of such writers as Shimmer Chinodya, Chenjerai Hove, Tsitsi Dangarembga, Yvonne Vera, and others. Chinodya's *Dew in the Morning* (1982) was the first Zimbabwean novel published during this period. Contrary to what one would have expected, it does not dwell on the political throes from which the country had just emerged. Rather, it depicts the struggles of a couple forced to live separate lives, the woman (Maziziva) living in the countryside and building a home singlehandedly, while her husband works and lives in the city where their children go to school. It further disappoints readers by its failure to explore the social and political pressures that force such a lifestyle on the couple and millions like them. His second novel, *Farai's Girls* (1984), follows the same pattern. Set in the 1970s when the freedom struggle was raging, the novel traces the amorous adventures of the libertine Farai and his many sexual encounters, blissfully discounting the nationalist war raging in the country. *Harvest of Thorns* (1991) breaks with the earlier two, though. Through the experiences of the hero, Benjamin (Pasi), it offers readers a view of the liberation war that acknowledges unheroic behavior among the freedom fighters, including the raping of fellow combatants.

Tsitsi Dangarembga's *Nervous Conditions* (1988), a work especially beloved of Western feminists, is also impressive for its choice of focus—on a young woman's consuming hunger for colonial education—and virtually absolute indifference to the momentous political developments rocking the country. The story centers around Tambudzai, a young girl whose infatuation with Western education is briefly frustrated by her parents' and uncle's decision to give priority to her older brother Nhamo's education. The men's main explanation is the familiar, but by no means frivolous or groundless, argument that education being the means to future financial security, Nhamo deserves the first and best shot at it, inasmuch as the welfare and well-being of the extended family will eventually depend on him as the oldest male. Nhamo's sudden and premature death removes him from the scene and Tambu realizes her dream. Recalling her brother's death later, she proclaims, "I was not sorry when my brother died. Nor am I apologising for my callousness . . . my lack of feeling."[9] Her closest association throughout the story is with her cousin Nyasha, approximately the same age as Tambu, but highly intelligent and sensitive. Having been raised in England, she has had opportunities to reflect upon and understand the cultural violence that colonialism and colonial education represent for Africans. But Nyasha's anguish at what she has lost through westernization leaves no mark on Tambu as she cheerfully pursues her goal of being the exemplary ward of colonial agents.

The timing of the events the largely autobiographical novel documents is significant, as much so as the author's scant attention to them. They coincide with Ian Smith's 1965 Unilateral Declaration of Independence (UDI), which set in motion the developments that will lead directly to the outbreak of the *chimurenga*. The novel insistently reduces practically all the strife in traditional society (one might say African society in general) to the effects of malignant African patriarchy, and it has won great favor among international champions of women's rights, who laud it as "a triumph for women's writing as well as for Zimbabwean literature."[10]

In contrast to the indifference of the foregoing work to the country's recent political upheaval, Chenjerai Hove's attention in his novels—in particular *Bones* (1988), the highly successful work which won the 1989 Noma Award for Publishing in Africa, and *Shadows* (1991)—is riveted on it. Both novels deal with the experience of the Zimbabwean people during colonialism and the difficult period after the successful struggle for independence. Both also adopt a richly evocative poetic style whose cadence, rhythm, and use of proverbs and other figures of speech closely approximates traditional verbal practice. In the following passage, Marume, whose spirit has been beaten out of him by the harshness of servile work on a white man's farm, excuses his tendency to care only for his stomach to his wife, Marita:

> One's stomach is one's ancestor. Where would one be without a good stomach? Do they not say that one day, mouth, stomach, hand and foot engaged in a senseless argument about who was king? But when nose discovered the argument, he also refused to smell the food for them. Things could not work out well for the stomach. The eyes began to cry and the hands became weak, so weak that a mere fly could have made them collapse. Then an agreement was reached, and all worked well then. But stomach kept on rumbling and roaring like a lion to make sure that all kept hearing stomach's presence. This is why mouth thought of the saying that one's stomach is one's ancestor.[11]

He continues: "I may not be able to move it, but when a river flows near my crops, I see it. . . . Some things are for the mouth. . . . Other things are for the eyes only. A river cannot flow for ever. Seasons leave room for one another."[12]

Hove's nod toward tradition and the past (which his style implies) does not, however, extend to his theme and message. *Bones* in particular is an assault on ancestors and traditional authority in general. Hove's message is that the ancestors slept on their watch when Europeans came to steal their land, and irresponsibly permitted the despoilers to alienate what was entrusted to them for safekeeping for posterity. At the center of the story are two heroic women, Marita and Janifa, the young woman Marita's son intends to marry if and when he returns from the forest, where he went "to go and learn how to fight without running away as [the] ancestors did."[13] Both women are employed, in the meantime, in virtual slave labor on a farm owned by Manyepo, a mean, abusive, and exploitative white farmer.

The African men on the farm, especially Marume, are spineless weaklings who cower under Manyepo's whip and berate Marita for standing up to the man, thus inviting more trouble for them. Traditional gender roles are reversed: Marita manfully confronts and defies the exploiter, while the men submit and whine. What's more, Marume complains that the ancestors who had not fought to keep the land from the grasp of the Europeans were like homeowners who abandoned their homes in fear of snakes on the roof:

> Does a man run away from his hut simply because a big snake has been seen on the roof? A man must fight the snake until it leaves his house or he kills it. To run away is to say to the snake, you are king. You are king, so you can go ahead and rule. That is not good for the ancestors. Any mother of such a person would wish she had not had her breast suckled by such a son.[14]

As a further instance of role reversal, it is Marita who assumes the duty of protecting the welfare of the family: when their son fails to return from the forest after four years, she sneaks off the farm and goes to the city to find out about him, and loses her life in the quest.

Hove's attack in this work extends beyond ancestors to current patriarchs. In this regard Hove makes Janifa's mother into an honorary patriarch in her understanding of her role as mother. She connives with Chisaga, facilitating his rape of Janifa, simply so she can get some cows from him to eat. The catalogue of depraved men continues when the herbalist (also named Marume) Janifa's parents hire to take care of the hemorrhage that resulted from her rape insists on taking his turn having sex with her.

Bones takes place against the backdrop of the fight to recover the land from the settlers, while its sequel, *Shadows*, is the story of two youths who commit suicide because adults will not sanction their love for each other. Its backdrop is the intra-African (Shona versus Ndebele) fighting that plagued Zimbabwe after its attainment of independence, but the seeds of the problem were sown during the time of white domination. The heroine is Johana; her father had abandoned his home in Gutu, where the land was poor, and had accepted better land from the whites in Gotami's land (the land of the descendants of Gotami) to farm according to their directives. The move also enabled him to avoid paying material tribute to Gutu's chief. But in his new home, apart from facing problems with the unfamiliar climate, flora, and fauna, he is also in trouble with the gods, whose name he does not know how to invoke, and with the "dizdents" (dissidents), who accuse him and his family of selling out.

Johana's tragedy results from her being separated from the Gutu cohort among whom she would have found a mate. In Gotami's land she lacks suitors, and engages in indiscreet sex with Marko, her father's hired hand and protégé, who is several years her junior. When her father discovers the resulting pregnancy he attempts to kill the offending Marko. In the confusion and misinformation that ensue the young lovers commit suicide in circumstances that recall the tragedy of Romeo and Juliet.

While in *Bones* Hove portrays the ancestors involved in an unheroic light, other writers represent them as fighting gamely against formidable odds and giving up their lives in their refusal to concede their huts to invading snakes. One such writer is Solomon M. Mutswairo, author of the historical novel *Mapondera: Soldier of Zimbabwe* (1978). Mapondera, the hero of the story, was a contemporary of the famed medium Nehanda, who is credited with ordering the first *chimurenga* against English settlers and who was hanged in 1898 for her resistance. Mutswairo's work is not great literature, but it is a patriot's homage to the sacrifices of his Shona forebears who, though vanquished by superior force and cunning, deserve the reverence of their descendants. He documents Mapondera's justified wariness in his dealing with Frederick Courtney Selous, Cecil Rhodes's agent, in 1889, and the perfidious exploitation of the resulting "contract" by the British as a ruse for imposing their rule on the land they would later name Rhodesia. Mapondera was a powerful warrior and a medium, reputedly capable of remarkable feats in battle, including taking to the air and flying about like a winged serpent. He scored some resounding victories against the settlers, and presumably would have kept them on the defensive had he not left his people at a crucial moment in 1898 to help the Makombe fight off the Portuguese in what later became Mozambique.

Mapondera returned to mount some resistance against the settlers, but the Africans were vanquished, disunited, and dispirited. He was caught, tried, and sentenced to prison in 1904, and the total victory of the whites seemed assured. But, with a sure sense of history, Mutswairo notes that his fight (and Nehanda's) is the same one that later flared up again in the second *chimurenga*: "What appeared to have been a quiet period [for the settlers] was only a period of respite due to the suppression of the people's aspirations through totalitarian oppression. . . . The uneasy peace of the settlers over the years has turned out to be that of Zimbabwe Invictus—The Victorious Zimbabwe."[15] Since the same author wrote the pioneering *Feso*, which enjoyed the colonizers' imprimatur, one can say that he redeemed himself (if he needed redemption) with *Mapondera*.

Yvonne Vera is one of the newest arrivals on the Zimbabwe literary scene, but one who has already established herself as a voice to reckon with, having won the Commonwealth Writers Prize (Africa Region) for her novel about incest, *Under the Tongue* (1997). She has other books to her credit, including *Nehanda* (1995), about Nehanda, "an offspring of the earth." The crux of Vera's version of the story can be seen as Nehanda's adoption of the colonizers' weapon, the gun, as a means of resisting them, that is, adopting the very symbol of change as a means of resisting change.[16] Despite appearances to the contrary (at the time) the strategy does succeed, because the people of Zimbabwe, having learned to use the colonizers' weapons, eventually threw off the colonial yoke.

A later novel by Vera is *Butterfly Burning* (2000), in which she gives free rein to a virtuoso's flair for the English language, which at times calls Wole Soyinka to mind, and at others Toni Morrison. *Butterfly Burning* is also remarkable in moving away from preoccupation with the recent political problems in the country to concentrate instead on human, interpersonal relationships. It does not entirely ignore politics, though, for part of understanding Fumbatha's character is knowing that his father was one of seventeen men the white settler government of Rhodesia hanged in 1896, and that he now copes with the harsh living conditions African workers endure in the country's version of apartheid. But the main action of the story revolves around a young woman's problems of reconciling her gender role with her career ambition.

Phephelaphi is involved in a romantic relationship with the much older Fumbatha, but she also wants to study nursing. The involvement is incompatible with that ambition, because she knows Fumbatha will object. In the end she becomes pregnant with his child, and the nursing school prefers strictly single women, not married ones, and certainly not expectant ones. Her opting to protect her nursing school admission by self-induced abortion costs her Fumbatha's love, and eventually her own life.

The story offers ample opportunities for Vera to dwell on the supposed perversity of the patriarchal system that established and maintains a social arrangement that can lead to the untimely death of young women like Phephelaphi. Although she seizes such an opportunity (but without stridency) in *Opening Spaces: An Anthology of Contemporary African Women's Writing* (1999), a collection of women's short stories she edited, in *Butterfly Burning*

Vera refrains from taking a blinkered view of the situation. In narrating the unfortunate woman's story Vera calls into question the institutional prejudices against married or expectant women, implemented to ensure efficiency through policies devised by bureaucrats who could have been men or women.

Opening Spaces is Vera's contribution to the African feminist cause, her testimony to the fact that "women from African have not been swallowed by history, that they too know how to swallow history," and also to the fact that "Africa has erred in its memory."[17] The stories by women from across the continent cover the gamut of types and experiences of women, showing, above all, that attempts to construct a unified feminine experience in the continent, or anywhere for that matter, are delusory at best.

Among other works of interest are Vera's *Without a Name* (1994), about Mazvita's futile attempt to find freedom in the anonymity of the city; Sekai Nzenza-Shand's *Songs to an African Sunset* (1997), an insightful exposé on life in a changing Zimbabwe; Edmund O.Z. Chipamaunga's *Chains of Freedom* (1998), about the post-independence struggles of Gono and Tapi, a couple of ex-combatants; and Chinodya's *Can We Talk, and Other Stories* (1998), which deals with a variety of social and human problems.

In addition to fiction, several African writers have produced autobiographies, many dealing with the struggle for independence, among them Joshua Nkomo, whose work is entitled *The Story of My Life.* The controversy that attended his life continues even after his death: on August 4, 2001, Zimbabwe Newspapers, the government-controlled publishers of the *Chronicle* (Harare), fired its editor, Steve Mpofu, for heavily censoring large sections of the biography, which the paper was serializing. As many as 1,385 words had been deleted from the text.[18]

Poetry

Little significant poetry came from the country through the early 1970s. A burst of poetic activity occurred, though, from the late 1970s, with the emergence of poets like Hopewell Seyaseya, Albert Chimedza, Chenjerai Hove, and F. E. Muronda. Writing in circumstances similar to those which inspired the poetry of South African poets like Dennis Brutus, they composed poems "from the center of the broken dream of the present"[19] about their people's suffering under white misrule and their hope for a new tomorrow that would be ushered in by revolutionary struggle. The ex-combatant Freedom T.V. Nyamubaya, who fought in the Zimbabwe National Liberation Army, writes poems that refer constantly to her military experience. She testifies to the resilience and survival of the enemy even after the end of the military campaign, although in a less recognizable form, saying that she must therefore continue the struggle, but aim her guns at different targets.

Chimedza's poetry, which a critic has described as "self-indulgent and out of control, an unstructured, undisciplined hallucination marked by the gratuitous use of shocking language,"[20] aligns him with the equally out of control and shocking Dambudzo Marechera, who uses earthy language to describe himself in the poem "Identify the Identity Parade."

Perhaps the most accomplished among the poets is Chenjerai Hove, who writes in both Shona and English. He achieved fame with *Red Hills of Home* (1985), which, although published after independence, is suffused with the pain and anguish of the era of white domination and abuse. His more recent *Rainbows in the Dust* (1998) is a testimony to the shift in public concern since independence, from white oppression to African self-misgovernment. The message of one of the longer poems, "I will not speak," is that of enforced silence in the face of horrendous wrongs, "when the presidential speech spills blood" and the like. The catalogue of ills continues, the poet repeatedly announcing his refusal (or inability) to speak, even at the end.

The collection is somewhat pan-African in scope, for it deals with the state of anomie not only within his country but in the entire continent. The poem "Apartheid" refers to the infamous system that institutionalized racial bigotry in South Africa, but does so in a humorous way. Other poems in the collection also deal with South Africa, among them "flower (a poem for south africa, 1995)" and "rainbow (for south africa, 1995)" while "on the death of ken saro-wiwa (november 10, 1995)" concerns the execution of the Nigerian poet Ken Saro-Wiwa on the orders of the Nigerian dictator Sani Abacha.

Drama

Drama is far less developed in Zimbabwe than the other literary genres. In fact, there was little to speak of until after independence. The country's best-known playwright, Stephen Chifunyise, began his literary career in Zambia in the late 1960s, writing for stage, radio, and television. After independence he published *Medicine for Love and Other Plays* (1984), a collection of plays that deal more with social and domestic problems than with the country's dramatic political experience.

Media

Zimbabwe has both electronic (radio and television) and print (newspaper) media, with the government and private interests offering services. The government's involvement in the electronic area takes the form of the Zimbabwe Broadcasting Corporation, which operates four radio channels (Radios One, Two, Three, and Four) and two television channels. In the print area the government's agency is Zimbabwe Newspapers, Ltd.

Electronic Media

Radio   The Zimbabwe Broadcasting Corporation (ZBC) is independent Zimbabwe's inheritor of a broadcasting legacy that dates to the period before World War II. Amateur radio broadcasting in the country began in 1933, with relaying of BBC programming for the most part, in an English-language service catering to the white community. In 1941 the colonial government inaugurated commercial broadcasting when it built a studio in Salisbury (Harare) and employed a professional staff; the programs continued to be in English. During the period of federation in the 1950s, the federation government took control, and in 1958 it created the Federal Broadcasting Corporation (FBC), which, on the dissolution of the federation in 1963, became the Southern Rhodesian Broadcasting Corporation (SRBC), and later the Rhodesian Broadcasting Corporation (RBC). After independence the RBC became the ZBC.

The ZBC provides programming on both short wave and FM. The FM stations broadcast in stereo, but the facilities of the Posts and Telecommunications Corporation, which controls the country's airwaves, can only deliver monaural signals. Radio One caters to the adult English-speaking population with offerings that include news, music, light entertainment, sports, comedy, discussions, quizzes, and dramas. Radio Two broadcasts in Shona and Ndebele to an African audience. Its offers dramas, features, and discussions on social, cultural, sporting, and economic issues. It also programs music that is predominantly Zimbabwean. Radio Three plays popular music for the young, and also offers some information and education. Radio Four, the educational channel, cooperates closely with the Ministry of Education's Audio Services and other government agencies to deliver formal and nonformal educational broadcasts to both young and adult listeners. Most of its broadcasts are in Shona, Ndebele, and English, but the minority languages Chewa, Tonga, Venda, Kalanga, and Shangani each receive ninety minutes of air time every week. Apart from Radio Three, which is on the air twenty-four hours a day, the rest broadcast from 5:00 A.M. until midnight daily.

Television   In 1963 the Rhodesian government bought out the private owners of a commercial television company serving Salisbury, and later expanded its services to Bulawayo, Gweru, and Mutare. By the end of the 1970s television programming was reaching most of the country, patronized mainly by the white population. Today the ZBC serves just over half of the population through TV One, a commercial station that broadcasts nationally, offering its viewers live and prerecorded shows: news, public affairs, soap operas, cartoons, music, comedies, feature films, and magazine and talk shows. TV One goes on the air on weekdays at 6:00 A.M. and breaks at 9.00 A.M., resumes at 3.15 P.M., and closes down at midnight. On the weekends it broadcasts continuously from 6:00 A.M. until midnight.

Complementing the services of TV One is TV Two, a private station operated by Flame Lily Broadcasting (Pvt.) Ltd.'s Joy TV. It started operating in July 1997 in studio facilities it leases from ZBC, and broadcasts to viewers within a radius of approximately 75 to 90 miles around Harare. It plans to extend its services to Bulawayo in the near future. Its programming includes live sports, dramas, comedies, music, and thrillers, and it features imported programs like *Sunset Beach, The Young and the Restless, Friends, ER,* and *Jenny Jones.* A 1999 survey showed that ZBC's TV One attracts 52 percent of television viewers to Joy TV's 37 percent. South African and other sources split the remainder.[21]

Newspapers

Newspaper publication began in the 1890s with European occupation. Most of the publications served only local interest, and few lasted very long. The Rhodesian Printing and Publishing Company, a subsidiary of South Africa's Argus Group, owned and operated the most substantial and durable. These were the *Rhodesia Herald, Sunday Mail, Bulawayo Chronicle, Sunday News,* and *Umtali Post.* There were a few smaller papers, like the *Gwelo Times* and the *Fort Victoria News.* Until the country's Unilateral Declaration of Independence (UDI) in 1965, the Argus Group of papers supported the government's policies, but after that they became critical of the government, a shift that incurred the latter's hostility and earned the papers persecution and censorship. In 1981, after independence, the new government bought the papers from Argus and established the Zimbabwe Media Trust to operate them. The trust in turn created Zimbabwe Newspapers, Ltd., as the publishers of the papers.

The country's major newspapers today are the *Herald,* a Harare-based daily, and the *Chronicle,* a Bulawayo-based daily, the *Manica Post,* which is based in Mutare and appears every Friday, Bulawayo's *Sunday News,* and Harare's *Sunday Mail.* All of the foregoing are part of Zimbabwe Newspapers (Pvt.) Ltd., and are partially funded by the government. In addition, the privately owned *Daily News* publishes from Monday to Friday, while the *Dispatch* and the *Eastern Star*, both part of the Associated Newspapers of Zimbabwe (ANZ) stable, are Friday weeklies. The privately owned *Zimbabwe Independent* and the *Zimbabwe Mirror*, the *Standard*, and the *Financial Gazette* are weeklies, the first two being Friday papers, the *Standard* a Sunday paper, and the *Gazette* a Thursday publication.

The Smith regime used the government-owned media explicitly to support Rhodesian Front policies. Initially, the radio was oriented toward the British Broadcasting Corporation, relaying BBC news and other programs, but when relations between Britain and Rhodesia became strained radio programming shifted its focus and dependence to the South African Broadcasting Corporation. The independent government has resorted to the same tactics the Smith regime used during its days in power—using the media to tout government policies and actions. As a result they have come under the scrutiny of the Media Monitoring Project (MMPZ), a joint initiative of the Zimbabwe chapter of the Media Institute of Southern Africa, the Catholic Commission for Justice and Peace in Zimbabwe, and Article 19 (the International Centre Against Censorship) which is based in Johannesburg and London. The MMPZ began monitoring all news and current affairs coverage in the publicly owned media—the Zimbabwe Broadcasting Corporation and Zimbabwe Newspapers (1980) Ltd.—in January 1999, and in June of that year it extended full monitoring to the private media as well.[22] It issues periodic reports as well as alerts when developments so warrant. Its findings indicate that the public is inadequately informed on issues of national importance.[23]

NOTES

1. A. C. Hodza and G. Fortune, comps. and eds., *Shona Praise Poetry* (Oxford: Oxford University Press, 1979), 27.
2. Ibid., 38–41.
3. Ibid., 6.
4. Ibid., 340.
5. E. W. Krog, ed., *African Literature in Rhodesia* (Gwelo, Zimbabwe: Mambo Press, in association with the Rhodesia Literature Bureau, 1966), 13.
6. Hodza and Fortune, 27.
7. Ibid., 25.
8. Krog, 13.
9. Tsitsi Dangarembga, *Nervous Conditions* (Seattle, WA: Seal Press, 1989), 1.
10. Barbara McCrea and Tony Pinchuck, *Zimbabwe and Botswana: The Rough Guide* (London: Rough Guide Ltd., 1996), 386.
11. Chenjerai Hove, *Bones* (Oxford: Heinemann, 1988), 30.
12. Ibid.

13. Ibid., 62.

14. Ibid., 86–87.

15. Solomon M. Mutswairo, *Mapondera, Soldier of Zimbabwe* (Washington, DC: Three Continents Press, 1978), 127.

16. Emilie Cassou, "Change in Yvonne Vera's *Nehanda*," www.scholars.nus.edu.sg/ landow/post/zimbabwe/vera/cassou3.html

17. Yvonne Vera, ed., *Opening Spaces: An Anthology of Contemporary African Women's Writing* (Oxford: Heinemann, 1999), 2.

18. *Daily News*, August 5, 2001, "Chronicle Editor Forced to Leave," www.dailynews. co.zw/daily/2001/July/July5/12004.html

19. Thomas Knipp, "English-Language Poetry," in *A History of Twentieth-Century African Literatures*, ed. Oyekan Owomoyela (Lincoln: University of Nebraska Press, 1993), 129.

20. Ibid.

21. Flame Lily Broadcasting (Pvt) System, "About Us," www.africaonline. co.zw/joytv/about.html

22. *Home Page* (Media Monitoring Project in Zimbabwe), "A Cog in the Democratic Wheel," www.wysiwyg://39/http://mmpz.icon.co.zw/index.html

23. Ibid.

4

Art, Cinema, and Architecture

ZIMBABWE'S ARTISTIC HERITAGE includes the ancient rock paintings that are scattered over wide areas of the country and the magnificent architecture of the Great Zimbabwe. The ancient sculptural skill evident in the so-called Zimbabwe birds found in the ruins of the Great Zimbabwe monument persists today in the works of numerous accomplished sculptors, some ranking among the best in the world. The people also demonstrate their creativity in their crafting of materials for everyday use: pots for cooking and water storage, fabrics (for which they employ fibers, grasses, and reeds), and headrests, to name a few. In this connection we might mention their habit of decorating their dwellings with artistic motifs.

SCULPTURE

Whereas sculpture abounds in some parts of Africa, for example as representations of gods, it is relatively uncommon in southern Africa, although groups like the Venda and the Thonga-Shangane do produce some figurative wood carvings. In general, material arts in southern Africa are functional and personal, rather than symbolic or decorative. While the Shona traditionally worked iron and carved wood figures, they did not produce masks or symbolic sculpture. The iron and wood objects were (and are) employed mainly in the contexts of male initiation (where they serve as visual aids in sexual instruction), divination, and healing. They are also used as household and field sentinels.

The presence of some stone sculpture, in particular of soapstone birds, at the Great Zimbabwe bears witness to an ancient tradition of sculpture among the Shona, and surviving artifacts from the area are also on display in museums in London and Cape Town. But the tradition has not survived to modern times, Zimbabwe's new, world-famous sculpture owing its beginning to the interest of mission school teachers who after World War II taught their pupils to carve wood reliefs and rounded figures. It received a further impetus from Frank McEwan, who as director of the Rhodesian Arts Gallery established the Central African Workshop in 1957 as a means of cultivating local artists.

McEwan started with five painters but soon built a larger studio to accommodate more painters and some sculptors, individuals who were previously employed in other pursuits as builders, dancers, farmers, museum workers, musicians, and policemen. He steered them toward the use of stone and the incorporation of spiritual and folkloric themes. In 1966 Tom Blomefield, a tobacco farmer and amateur carving enthusiast, started the Tengenenge Sculpture Community for his workers. Like McEwan, he too encouraged his carvers to work with stone and to use the medium to express ideas reminiscent of their traditional cultures. Since the artists included workers from Angola and Malawi in addition to Shona workers, the usual description of the products of the community as Shona sculpture is something of a misnomer.

Similar in purpose to Tengenenge is the Chapungu Sculpture Park, which is located on fifteen acres in the industrial area Msasa, less than a mile and a half from the center of Harare. It comprises an outdoor garden for displaying historical works, sales and exhibition galleries, an arena for artistic performances, and a refreshment area. With its natural rock formations, it offers outdoor studio facilities to artists, who receive year-long residential fellowships and material support, including tools, and encouragement to experiment and create. It began as the Gallery Shona in Harare in 1970, when Roy Guthrie sought to provide a working outlet for sculptors adversely affected by the war for independence; it thus complemented the Tengenenge Community as the only private galleries devoted to stone sculpture in the country. Its relocation in 1985 to the present site is an eloquent testimony to its success. Its early beneficiaries include Nicholas Mukomberanwa, Boira Mteki, Joseph Ndandarika, and Sylvester Mubayi.

Zimbabwe sculptors use rocks—serpentine, quartz, sandstone, verdite, granite, steatite, and others—that occur in abundance in the countryside, sometimes on the sculptors' own property. Their technology also varies, including heating, burnishing, texturing, and other methods, to bring out the best effects of the natural properties of the rocks. Their final products are sometimes stylized and sometimes realistic sculptures—animal and human forms, and also figures drawn from folklore and mythology.

International exhibitions of Zimbabwe sculpture have taken place since 1963, when McEwan arranged an exhibition at the Commonwealth Institute in London. The Museum of Modern Art in New York mounted a similar exhibition in 1968, as did the Museum Rodin of Paris in 1971. Since independence many more such exhibitions have occurred, featuring both Tengenenge and Chapungu. In 1981 Chapungu sculptors featured in an exhibition at Zimbabwe House in London, and in one-man shows of Mukomberanwa's and Henry Munyaradzi's works, respectively, at the Commonwealth Institute in 1983 and 1984.

Bernard Matemera's work won a major award in India in 1986, and in the 1990s Zimbabwe sculptors were featured at a number of exhibitions and galleries, including Contemporary African Artists: Changing Tradition (Studio Museum, Harlem, New York, 1990); Venice Biennale (1991); Africa 95 (London, 1995); and Reece Gallery (New York, 1996), the last highlighting the works of Tapfuma Gutsa. During 2000 Chapungu displayed some of its monumental stone sculptures, some weighing as much as 6,000 pounds and standing as tall as ten feet, at the Royal Botanical Gardens at Kew (Kew Gardens) in England, and later, from April to October 2001, at the Missouri Botanical Gardens in St. Louis.

Nicholas Mukomberanwa, who was honored in 1986 by the country's president, Robert Mugabe, for his contributions to the art, earned the reputation of being the dean of Zimbabwe sculptors. Other notable Zimbabwe sculptors whom critics rank among the best in the world are Joram Mariga (one of McEwan's original wards, who began as a wood-carver but later switched to stone), Sylvester Mubayi, Joseph Ndandarika, Tapfuma Gutsa, Maxwell Gochera, Bernard Matemera, and John Takawira.

WOOD CARVING

Traditionally, wood carving is a male occupation, and often a family or lineage pursuit, although sometimes an aspiring artist from a noncarving family may undertake to learn the trade. Today wood-carvers, some of them specialists, produce a variety of items, such as doors, figures, bowls, drums, xylophones, mortars, stools, staffs, and milk pails. Among some groups, the Venda for example, only chiefs use wood carvings, and then only in their capitals. These carvings, as well as the wooden keys of the xylophones played on special occasions, are often decorated. Large doors with crocodile designs (the symbol of chiefship) identify the chief's own sleeping hut, and large hemispherical drums whose upper panels are similarly decorated symbolize his rainmaking powers.

While the use of wood carvings is in general a restricted preserve of chiefship, divination trays enjoy an exception, but then divination is somehow linked to the courts: diviners use the trays to detect witches or the chiefdom that harbors a witch. Furthermore, some healers use carved wooden containers for their medicines, while some diviners use them to represent their patron spirits. The jointed puppets common in the area, people believe, probably originated among the Thonga and spread to neighboring countries through the agency of itinerant Thonga diviners and healers.

Also enjoying an exception to the chiefly monopoly are the Venda matrons who instruct young women undergoing initiation on social and sexual mores, and instill ethnic identity into them. They are permitted to use representative carvings at the final stages of the initiation process.

Although the most famous Zimbabwe figurative artists tend to be those who work in stone, some wood-carvers have also produced exquisite sculptures. One of the best is Barnabas Ndudzo, who is famous for his full-sized naked human figures as well as striking realistic and expressive busts. His son Shepherd is also an accomplished sculptor.

Headrests

Headrests, or carved wooden pillows, are common among southern African cultures, and they have so fascinated European visitors and collectors that they are the most familiar form of Shona sculpture in Europe. Available evidence suggests that gold-plated headrests were in use at Khami in the sixteenth and seventeenth centuries. The Shona headrest is usually smaller than the Zulu-Nguni version; it usually consists of an oval base and a carved piece (suggesting a female figure, and specifically the pubic area) connecting and supporting a curved platform for resting the head. Another difference is that whereas the Shona support suggests a female figure, the Nguni one usually represents a bull. One sometimes finds a Shona support that represents an animal, but in such cases the animal is usually a cow, antelope, or goat. Another feature of Shona headrests that is consistent with the female emphasis is their incorporation of protrusions that suggest breasts.

Shona men receive headrests on initiation to symbolize their new status, and these often become closely identified with their owners. Another symbolic use is to represent and invoke ancestors. The Shona believe that when a sleeping person dreams he or she is visiting the ancestors, the sources of knowledge and prosperity. When one wishes to communicate with an ancestor, therefore, one might take out the headrest the ancestor used when alive and address it. Alternatively, such a person might sleep on the headrest in the hope that doing so will effect the desired contact. Mediums also use headrests to invoke their patron spirits. The female (or sexual) features (the pubic area and the breasts) are also somehow connected to the ancestors, inasmuch as they are the source of fertility. The Shona conceive of the womb as a sacred pool, and along with the breasts it represents the ancestral realm. The imagery of the pubic area supposedly represents lovemaking (the act of child-making) as the throwing of a pebble into a pool, thus causing ripples which will alert the ancestors to their task of providing a child to continue the lineage.

In practical terms, owners of headrests might travel with them, especially when they are incorporated with other functional objects such as snuff containers and walking staffs, or might leave them at their doors to indicate that they are home. A husband with more than one wife might place his headrest at the door of the hut of the wife he wishes to spend the night with. Nowadays they are not as much in use as they once were, their main function, apart from those indicated above, being as heirlooms.

Staffs

Although sometimes combined with headrests, staffs are more likely to be free-standing. They are in common use by men and women in southern Africa (including Zimbabwe), diviners and healers being especially fond of them. They often function as status symbols, the length and extent of decoration indicating the height of the owner's standing. Such decorations vary; sometimes the tops take the shape of a human head, and sometimes snakes adorn the stem.

Snuffboxes

Snuffboxes are often carved from wood, but gourds and horns are also possible materials. The boxes are sometimes simply conical containers with simple stoppers, but often the container itself and the stopper may be shaped like an animal and otherwise decorated. Men and women use snuffboxes, and they also function in rituals to hold snuff for offering to the ancestors, or to facilitate spirit possession.

IRONWORK

In keeping with the gender division of artistic labor in southern Africa, ironworking is an important male specialty, supported by a local smelting technique that was developed to a high degree in the past, but that has been substantially lost in the course of the twentieth century. As a result of the loss of the smelting technology, the ironworking that takes place today depends on scrap metal instead of smelted iron. Ironworkers, or blacksmiths, manufacture utilitarian and personal items like knives (including ceremonial ones), hoe blades, and the like, but their most important product is the ceremonial axe known as the *gano*. Its crescent-shaped or semicircular blade is connected to a wooden handle by a narrow shank. Traditionally used for hunting elephants and in battle, the *gano* function now only as religious paraphernalia, often carried by spirit mediums.

Artists like Arthur Azevedo, Adam Madebe, and Ndebe (David) Ndlovu (b. 1963) have produced work in metal. Among the best known female sculptors in this medium are Agnes Nyanhongo and Locardia Ndandarika (b. 1945).

POTS, BARK CLOTHS, AND BASKETS

Women's art includes the manufacture of clay pots for different uses, waistbands and aprons, bark cloths, as well as floor and wall decorations. Women also manufacture baskets, although they do not have a monopoly in this case, for men also engage in the activity. The women make pots meant for initiation (sometimes to illustrate sexually explicit stories) from red clay; these are unbaked, and are usually destroyed after the ceremony. They make other, larger pots for cooking, storing drinking water, holding beer, or serving food. They often decorate such pots with bands of geometric designs, either painted on or etched into the clay.

Women also weave waistbands, aprons, and blankets from bark cloth, whose threads they manufacture from the softened inner bark of trees. These they weave by hand to make the desired articles of clothing.

OTHER MEDIA

In addition to the foregoing, the type of low-relief wood carving that the mission school teachers introduced after World War II has persisted, featuring such artists as Cornelius Manguma, Joseph Muli (b. 1944), Barnabas Ndudzu, and David Mutasa. Their patronage comes mainly from people interested in religious articles and African curios. In the 1980s and 1990s some artists like Tapfuma Gutsa, Richard Jack, Joseph Muzondo, Zephania Tshuma (b. 1932), and Morris Tendai began to work with new materials.

PAINTING

This is another medium in which the expertise evident in relics of the Zimbabwe past has not survived to modern times. Whereas the area is world famous for its magnificent rock paintings, like those in the Matopo Hills, modern Zimbabwe painting goes back only to the mid-nineteenth century. White painting dating from this period typically expresses the settlers' apprehension of their environment and response to it, and the extent to which the small white community felt awed by the vast and imposing landscape with its majestic physical features. By contrast, Africans' painting, from about the middle of the twentieth century, reflects the condition of the African population—the harshness of life, urban crime, domestic problems, and drought, but also the vibrancy of city life. Notable among the painters are George Nene (b. 1959), a veteran of the *chimurenga,* and Louis Meque (b. 1966), who studied at the arts workshop of the National Gallery.

CINEMA

Zimbabwe's cinema legacy dates back to the Colonial Film Unit that the government of Great Britain created at the beginning of World War II for propaganda purposes, and later to promote community development and health in the colonies. After the Rhodesian Front came to power in the country in 1962, the role of the descendant film unit, now under the Ministry of Information, became the promotion of the ideologies of the minority white racist government. When the armed struggle for African liberation began, the screen became a combatant on the white side against African guerrilla fighters and the entire African community. The films it produced, often blood-curdling in their violence and crudeness, were designed to intimidate the African support base for the fighters. Perhaps the worst of them was the untitled "hyena film": it shows hyenas eating the remains of three dead guerrilla fighters who, after receiving some help from villagers, had apparently been killed by government forces. The lingering shots of the animals devouring human brains and pulling out human entrails revolted the African audiences much more than the arrest of the villager-helpers intimidated them, and the government's strategy backfired.

After independence the government made an attempt to develop a thriving commercial film industry based on the Hollywood model, and in fact engaged in a joint venture with Universal Studios to produce *Cry Freedom* (1987). The failure of the venture persuaded the government to shift its interest to sponsoring short documentaries on educational and social matters through the Production Services unit of the Ministry of Information. Lack of adequate funding has, however, severely limited the unit's impact. Independent filmmakers funded by donors from outside the country have been more successful, and have produced some quite memorable features. In keeping with the preferences of the donors, such films have focused on pressing social problems and the need to correct them.

Jit (1990), the first film made in Zimbabwe with local financing and local production, was a big hit. Directed by Michael Raeburn, it features some of the best musicians in the country on its sound track, and also carries an entertaining storyline. It is the story of the love of UK, the hero, for Sofi, a gangster's girlfriend, and the problems her father's demand for a hefty bride-price poses. Other features focus on more serious social problems: *Neria* (1992) and *Flame* (1996) focus on the social inequities women face; *Everyone's Child* (1997) and *More Time* (1993) deal with AIDS and its consequences on society and social relations; and *Keep on Knocking* (1996) is about trade unions in the country.

In *Neria*, the heroine (whose name the film bears) and her husband are a successful couple who live in Harare. Upon his sudden death, his mother wants Neria to leave her city job and return to the village. Both her mother-in-law and her brother-in-law (Phineas) want to keep the couple's wealth in the family—by making Neria marry Phineas, as custom permits. The plot allows the director, Godwin Nawuru, and his collaborator, Tsitsi Dangarembga, to editorialize cinematically on wife inheritance, to them yet another feature of African patriarchy that bedevils women. In the end Neria's mother-in-law becomes enlightened and supports Neria's preference to remain a widow in the city.

Flame, which was funded by the European Union, won the Organization of African Unity Prize at the South African Film Festival in 1996. It recalls the abuse and rape women fighters endured at the hands of their male comrades during the second *chimurenga*, and their lack of recognition, in contrast to the men, in independent Zimbabwe.[1] A 1996 editorial in the *Sunday Mail* dismissed the film as "a work of sabotage designed to tarnish the image of the liberation movement and its central role in the death of Rhodesia and the birth of Zimbabwe."[2]

Everyone's Child is a star-studded production of the Media for Development Trust of Zimbabwe, which devotes itself to using the media to call attention to urgent social problems. The plot, about the consequences of AIDS fatality on the deceased's surviving children, is based on a story by the renowned author Shimmer Chinodya. The film was directed by the equally famous novelist and Zimbabwe's first female filmmaker, Tsitsi Dangarembga; its sound track features original compositions by leading Zimbabwe musicians, including Thomas Mapfumo, and it also features some of the country's best actors.

Various institutions and organizations have emerged in Zimbabwe to facilitate film production, including Africa Film and TV, the African Script Development Fund, the Film Training School (Harare), Framework International, Media for Development Trust, and Zimmedia. In 1996 women filmmakers formed their own organization, the Women Filmmakers of Zimbabwe, in order to ensure that "women's names sit next to tags like director, producer, editor, script writer when credits roll up the screen at the end of films."[3]

ART SPONSORSHIP

Zimbabwe art has received support and encouragement from church missions, which in many cases provided the pioneering impetus for modern artistic traditions. As an example, the Cyrene Mission at Matopo Hills (founded in 1939) began to offer art education to young artists, encouraging them to paint and sculpt works with Christian motifs. The government has also actively promoted the arts through the National Gallery of Zimbabwe in Harare, which mounts several exhibitions of local artists annually, and through the National Arts Council. Additional private sponsorship comes from the diplomatic community, hotels, and individuals. There are also several galleries, including Gallery Delta (founded 1975), Gallery Shona Sculpture (1972), Matambo Gallery (1985), Stone Dynamic (1987), Tengenenge Sculpture Community (1966), Vhukutiwa Gallery (1992), and the French Embassy's gallery at Le Forum (1974). Art education became a part of the school curriculum in 1980, and advanced instruction is available at Harare Polytechnic (1963), Mzilikazi Art and Craft Centre (1963), Bulawayo (1963), and the National Gallery's Workshop School (1962; after 1981 the BAT Workshop School) in Harare. The residential Tengenenge Sculpture Community remains active, and since 1988 the country has sponsored Pachipamwe (Work Together) international workshops.

ARCHITECTURE AND HOUSING

The Great Zimbabwe

The country Zimbabwe is so named in order to enshrine its people's continuity with the Rozvi kingdom that erected the Great Zimbabwe. The magnificence of the feat its builders accomplished requires that any discussion of Zimbabwe architecture acknowledge it, even if the ancient builders did not bequeath their skill to their descendants. A few words about its construction are therefore in order.

The Hill Ruins, a complex of walls, boulders, and enclosures in which the builders skillfully incorporated existing boulders into wall formations, have always awed visitors with their exquisite and magnificent architectural features. The walls themselves are built with blocks of granite rocks gathered

from the surrounding hills that occur naturally in parallel slabs that are easily cut into the required sizes. These the architects arranged in such a way
that they stay in place without the need of mortar between blocks or at
wall junctions. Moreover, the builders achieved their feat without building
foundations.

The earliest walls (representing most of the Hill Ruins) are of rough
blocks arranged in irregular layers. Later walls were built of well-dressed and
carefully laid stone blocks, arranged in close, well-matched, and regular layers. The same style is to be found in the Elliptical Building's outer wall and
conical tower. Later still came a style representing a decline in skill, with the
stones laid at random, loosely fitted, and ill matched. There are also remnants of a later, even less skilled assemblage of crude stones.

The Western Enclosure is elliptical in shape and is more than 750 feet (250
meters) in circumference. Its outer walls are more than 33 feet (11 meters) tall
in some places, and up to 18 feet (5½ meters) thick. By itself it is reputedly
the largest stone structure ever constructed in sub-Saharan Africa.[4] Within
the great enclosure are smaller ones, walls punctuated by huge entrances sep-
arating the dwellings of the ruling class from the commoners. Scattered
about, usually at the entrances, are stone pillars, each of which is presumed
to have borne a family totem, marking the residential location of each family. The pillar at the royal residence bore the royal totem, the *zimbabwe* bird.
On the eastern side is an older inner wall separated from the outer one by a
narrow parallel passage, whose southern terminus is a conical tower, also
known as the Granary. The last designation is obviously a misnomer, for the
structure is solid from top to bottom.

Residential Arrangement

The residential areas comprised circular pole-and-*daga* huts (with low clay
walls and wooden posts that support thatched roofs) arranged around an
open courtyard. The open space is believed to have served as a firebreak, or
an opening where intruders or dangerous animals could be exposed. Stone
walls separated different family areas in the ruling class sector. At the heart
of each was the kitchen building with a hearth at its center, and, nearby, the
sleeping hut, whose walls were polished smooth, decorated, and often
painted. Inside it were furnishings, also molded from clay and polished.
These included sleeping platforms, seats, and so forth. In each household,
stepped platforms displayed the woman's household pots, which were of
great importance. The construction also provided special areas for livestock
and food storage. The granary was a hut raised about three feet off the
ground, as a precaution against insects, rodents, and dampness, and all its

surfaces were thoroughly plastered. Chicken coops were usually also on stilts, and cattle and goats were kept in kraals. Another important feature of the residential area was the *dare*, the meeting place (often in the shade of a tree) for discussing family or communal matters. Most of the *daga* huts have collapsed or have become overgrown with vegetation.

Traditional Domestic Architecture

Nothing in contemporary domestic architecture in Zimbabwe lives up to the grandeur of the Great Zimbabwe. The use of tall grasses as a natural fence around a village at the Chapungu Sculpture Park prompted a visitor to comment that "like the Hill Complex at Great Zimbabwe, this structure skillfully employs natural and manmade elements to create a space for human beings."[5] The comment encapsulates the trajectory of native architectural development: from the great and exquisitely constructed stone walls of the Great Zimbabwe to a natural fence of tall grasses. On the other hand, since the stone walls of the ancient edifice contained within them mud huts with thatched roofs very much like the ones that are still in use in the rural parts of the country, one can argue that in this regard there has been no retrogression, no change, and that the zimbabwes were simply a historical aberration, a flash of genius that made a sudden appearance and spent itself within a relatively short period.

Zimbabwe homesteads have not changed much from the ones in the residential area of the Great Zimbabwe. The settlements, or villages, remain clusters of circular clay-and-stick huts with conical thatched roofs, each room having a specific function. Typically a person's home would consist of two huts, one for sleeping and the other for cooking. In the novel *Nervous Conditions* (discussed in chapter 3) Tambudzai's description of her home at the homestead offers an excellent picture of domestic architecture and organization in the 1960s.

> Our yard contained many buildings which all had a specific purpose for our day to day living: the pole and *dagga* [*sic*] kitchen, which was . . . round; the *tsapi*, which was small . . . ; the *hozi*, where Nhamo [her late brother] had slept during the holidays that he did come home; and the House, which was built of red brick, had glass windows and a corrugated-iron roof.[6]

The house was considered special because of its red brick, glass windows, and corrugated iron roof, but also because it had a living room large enough for dining furniture, sofa, and armchair.

Nowadays the walls are often built of sun-dried bricks that are precisely coursed, and with rectangular, lintelled doorways and thatched roofs. Alongside such structures, one often sees rectangular buildings with brick or concrete block walls and corrugated iron roofing, a result of European influence. The walls may be decorated with simple geometric designs, some of them carrying symbolic or religious meaning. Huts for storage purposes are less sturdy than residential or cooking huts; their walls are built with thin sticks and branches. Wrought iron fencing is also increasingly popular for decoration and security, and the practice of building raised sleeping platforms, seats, cooking hearths, and so forth using clay also persists.

Among the Tonga, most people maintain homes in the village compound as well as huts on their farms, which are at some remove from the village. The village residence is the "permanent" address, but as soon as the seedlings germinate, the farmhouse becomes the home for the rest of the growing season. These homes in the field are lean-tos built of wood and raised off the ground by stilts up to nine feet high, and access is by means of ladders. Although they appear flimsy, they are sturdy enough to support entire families.

Modern Architecture in Zimbabwe

Zimbabwe's modern architecture is no more a worthy successor to the Great Zimbabwe than domestic architecture is. The general consensus on this score is that modern Zimbabwe architecture displays nothing of the excellence that characterizes the Great Zimbabwe. The architects of the buildings in the cities have not created anything distinctive, any structure that might set them apart from cities on other continents.

Colonial residences in the urban suburbs (the low-density areas) were typical of British colonies: they were inspired by the bungalow style developed in British India, and were seldom customized for local conditions, a glaring departure from the African practice of harmonizing dwellings with the environment and disturbing nature as little as possible in their construction. The colonists' attempt to temper the effects of the hot climate through the choice of external wall color in fact only accomplished a jarring clash with the environment. The earliest colonial and missionary houses, built around the turn of the nineteenth century, were dried mud brick bungalows which the Europeans painted white, because they thought that white would have a cooling effect on the houses. Later on they switched to pastel colors, "cream, pale pink, pale blue, pale green,"[7] having become convinced that such colors would serve as well as white. For their African wards, like school teachers, they built houses of red brick, which they left unpainted either because they presumed that Africans preferred bright colors or because they could not afford to spend time painting them.

Commercial farmhouses were long Cape Dutch bungalows, while the churches were generally simple rectangular buildings, sometimes topped by towers, and sometimes decorated with wall murals or low-relief carvings. Public structures like hotels, government buildings, and urban shopping centers built up to the 1930s were elaborate, and have been variously described as "pure raj" (like the Victoria Falls Hotel, built in 1904), Italian Renaissance, Edwardian Imperial, late Victorian, and so forth. They are indistinguishable from structures in other countries—"Singapore's Raffles, Bombay's Taj Mahal, and Capetown's Mount Nelson . . . [and] buildings found in both Pall Mall and Regent Street, London, and throughout the territories of the former British Empire."[8]

Students of the development of modern architecture in Zimbabwe since the establishment of white presence in the area have identified a number of periods and styles. So-called "oxcart architecture" of painted brick and thatched roofs prevailed in the 1890s, followed by the structures dubbed "railway architecture." This style also used brick but was decorated with cast-iron ornaments, topped with corrugated iron, and fronted with plate glass. Later, red tile roofing (which was less noisy during rainstorms and radiated less heat in the sun) replaced the iron sheets. Railway architecture was prevalent up to World War I. It was modified in the 1920s and 1930s, owing to influences from South Africa, by the incorporation of steel windows, in what became known as the neoclassical style. In the late 1950s modernism emerged, featuring European-style tower blocks with colorful reflecting walls. A representative example of the style is the National Gallery, which was completed in 1957. Finally came the contemporary style; several architects now use local materials and incorporate local forms into their buildings. In many regards, though, just as Zimbabwe politics has been closely intertwined with that of South Africa, so its architecture reflects developments in the republic to the south, to the extent that commentators suggest that southern African architecture is a regional phenomenon, with Harare and Johannesburg as the twin centers.

Some architectural structures in the country are famous for a variety of reasons. The home of the architect Anthony Wales-Smith is noteworthy as one of the few colonial bungalows to take account of local conditions. Heroes Acre (1981), also in Harare, is an imposing monument honoring the heroes of the liberation struggle. Designed by Koreans, it comprises abstract monumental architecture, sculptures, and friezes. It is also a mausoleum for the heroes of the second *chimurenga*, both dead and yet to die. The

ZIMCOR Building in Harare (completed in 1993) features experimentation with dark facing-bricks and local hardwoods, while the Monomotapa Hotel (which dates to the 1970s) has meandering walls that recall the Great Zimbabwe "and thus the country's ancient architectural tradition."[9] The Sheraton Hotel and Harare International Conference Centre is "the country's most controversial post-independence building . . . a shimmering gilt glass slab of monumental proportions."[10]

NOTES

1. Kedmon Nyasha Hungwe, "Fifty Years of Film-Making in Zimbabwe," n.d. www.szs.net/kedmon-hungwe/film-making-in-zimbabwe.html
2. "The Wrong Flame," *Sunday Mail* (Harare), February 4, 1996, http://web. mit.edu/course/21/21f.853/africa-film/0087.html
3. Bella Matambanadzo, "Cinema-Zimbabwe: The New Story Tellers," October 1, 1996, http://web.mit.edu/course/21/21f.853/africa-film/0315.html
4. R. Kent Rasmussen and Steven C. Rubert, *Historical Dictionary of Zimbabwe*, 2nd ed. (Metuchen, NJ: Scarecrow, 1990), 405.
5. George P. Landow, "Indigenous Domestic Architecture in Zimbabwe," http://landow.stg.brown.edu/post/zimbabwe/art/architecture/huts.html
6. Tsitsi Dangarembga, *Nervous Conditions* (Seattle, WA: Seal Press, 1989), 61.
7. Ibid., 63.
8. George P. Landow, "Indigenous Domestic Architecture in Zimbabwe," http://landow.stg.brown.edu/post/zimbabwe/art/architecture/huts.html
9. Barbara McCrea and Tony Pinchuck, *Zimbabwe and Botswana: The Rough Guide* (London: Rough Guides Ltd., 1996), 68.
10. Ibid., 69.

These two sons of a distinguished police officer relax in the Zimbabwe sun of the Kapungu homestead in Jari. Courtesy of Sunny Leigh Kapungu.

Before this wealthy family was forced to go underground because of the political work of Greek Maswoswe (shown back row, left) to free Zimbabwe from British rule, his family poses before they depart to Zambia. Courtesy of Sunny Leigh Kapungu.

A Zimbabwean couple and their children pose for a family picture. Courtesy of Sunny Leigh Kapungu.

Jordan Maswoswe (middle) joins his brothers-in-law in rural Zimbabwe in the Kapungu Homestead in Jari. Courtesy of Sunny Leigh Kapungu.

Married couple Sunny and Jordan Maswoswe upon their arrival to Zimbabwe in 1988 to be joined in a Shona marriage, re-affirming the vows they took seven years before. Courtesy of Sunny Leigh Kapungu.

A man and his wife, in Zimbabwean attire, stand outside their home. Courtesy of Sunny Leigh Kapungu.

Inspired by the Shona marriage ceremony, a romantic couple indulges at the reception. Courtesy of Sunny Leigh Kapungu.

Kudzai Tongoona. Courtesy of Fungai Tongoona.

Zimbabwean Family. © CIDA/ACDI photo: Bruce Paton.

Zimbabwean grandmother in front of kitchen hut. Courtesy of Fungai Tongoona.

Tennis players. Courtesy of Fungai Tongoona.

Tennis players. Courtesy of Fungai Tongoona.

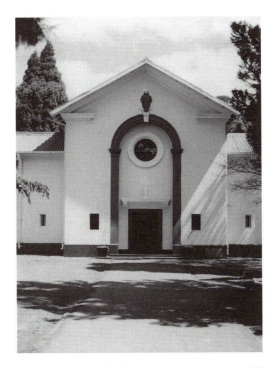

Memorial Chapel at Prince Edward School, Harare. Courtesy of Fungai Tongoona.

Prince Edward School, Harare. Courtesy of Fungai Tongoona.

5

Leisure, Dress, and Cuisine

LEISURE IN TRADITIONAL LIFE

TRADITIONAL ZIMBABWE SOCIETY can be justifiably, and undisparagingly, described as a beer culture, because of the high incidence of occasions that call for brewing and drinking beer. The people mark practically all memorable occasions and perform practically all rituals with a plentiful supply of beer, sometimes brewed ritualistically by specially designated people, and shared with the ancestors and the community as appropriate. The traditional calendar provided for holidays (*chisi*) during which work was suspended and people entertained themselves.

Today, it matters little whether one looks at rural communities where many of the old ways still persist, or at the urban centers, for one finds that however onerous the demands of making a living might be, and whatever the season, people find the time and some cause for the pursuit of pleasure. They even manage to turn eventualities that others might bemoan into occasions for having a party, for example, the *bira* which follows the unpleasant manifestation of ancestral displeasure, and at which through drinking, singing, and dancing, and the agency of a medium, the people coax the ancestors that are aggrieved to reveal the cause of his displeasure. At these celebrations no formal invitations are required to attend, for, with the exception of those rites and rituals that are open to initiates or closed groups only, every member of the society is welcome.

The elaborate efforts people devote to the social aspects of holidays and to rituals attending births, initiations, marriages, funerals, and the *bira*, especially the days devoted to brewing different kinds of beer, the actual feasting, the drumming, singing, and dancing, emphasize an acknowledgment of the necessity for balancing solemnity with festivity, for tempering the serious-ness of life with some play. This balanced approach to life is manifest in a variety of ways, not least in literature depicting the Shona experience. Solomon Mutswairo's fictionalized life of Mapondera, for example, bears witness to the assertion that even in times of tension and uncertainty the people still make room for merriment. In preparation for battle against the white settlers, Mapondera and other chiefs ordered a prewar celebration to last three days and coincide with "the Harvest Days Celebrations, and the *Huruva* days of grain threshing before the early spring rains of the *gukura-hundi.*"[1] The preparations—stretching the drums to the required tautness, preparing the food, brewing the beer, and so forth—occupied ten full days. The author gives the following account of the holiday festivities:

> The rest of the Harvest Celebrations were spent with much feasting, dancing and parading with old-fashioned rifles simulating battle scenes, and torch flames, reminiscent of the old Rozvi end-of-year cele-brations. . . . [A]ll night long the drums resounded and echoed the ec-stasy of the possessed dancers moving in their trances, singing their lungs out; some ripping open hens' and goats' throats and gulping down blood gushing from the animals' pulsating throats.[2]

Another traditional festival, the *marenje*, is held every January to implore the clan *mhondoro* (tribal spirit) for good rains for the planting season and for an abundance of crops. It is one of the three mandatory occasions when the people consult the spirit, the others being the naming of a new chief and in the event of a drought. What follows is a description of a *marenje* festival among the Korekore (MaKorekore).

In anticipation of the occasion, members of the community contribute finger millet for the beer required for the ceremonies. The *nechombo* (the medium's helper) receives the grains and arranges for the ritual brewing of the beer. The festivities begin with the playing of mbira music from early in the morning, when women dance the *mafuwe*, a ritual dance performed in a circle. After about two hours of music and dancing, the *nechombo* leads sev-eral men and two elderly women to the *mhondoro*'s shrine. The companions remain outside the shrine, while the *nechombo* enters and presents a pot of millet to the ancestral spirit, informing him that the people are preparing beer for him and are asking for good rain. The people waiting outside sec-ond his presentation, the men clapping and the women ululating.

Back at the village, the brewing of the beer is entrusted to a woman past childbearing. Ten days later, the chief, along with the *nechombo* and a clan elder, takes several pots of the beer to the shrine and presents them to the spirit, and the company shares one of the pots with the onlookers. Early the next morning, those who had contributed millet assemble, the beer is brought out of the shrine, and the people drink of it. The *nechombo*, the chief, and his ritual friend (*sahwira*) reenter the hut, remind the spirit that the beer has been brewed for him, and ask again for rain and protection from lightning. Again, the men waiting outside clap and the women ululate. The ceremonies conclude with the women again dancing the *mafuwe*.[3]

The quest for pleasure is not confined to such holiday occasions either, for the *dare*, the space for thrashing out weighty family or communal matters, is also a place for diversion, "a forum and sanctuary for men, where they can be free of female intrusion. . . . Men repair there early in the morning, sometimes before breakfast, to warm themselves before the fire, and sometimes to smoke *mbanje* (hemp)."[4] There are also always parties, *humwe* or *nimbi*, in their own village or a neighboring one.[5]

As for the youth, in the temporal spaces between ritual occasions, they occupy themselves with such diversions as bird-snaring (using birdlime) or the game of *nuri*. Opposing teams face each other across a pitch, and as the leader of one team sends a disk-shaped puck (made from a root) sliding toward the opponents, they attempt to spear it in motion with a wooden spear, the object being to impale it well enough to be able to lift it off the ground with the spear. Another means of diversion is the board game *mwari* (or *wari*), in which two players each control the side of a long board with several holes containing seeds on its two sides. Each player attempts, through different maneuvers, to capture more of the seeds than his opponent by the time the holes have been emptied of their contents. This game is popular in one variety or another throughout sub-Saharan Africa.

The modern counterparts of the traditional *chisi* are the national holidays, observances of a mix of rites and events, some established and sponsored by the defeated colonists, and others in celebration of their defeat. The year of national festivals begins on January 1, New Year's Day; next is Independence Day, which is April 18; Workers' Day falls on May 1, and Africa Day on May 25; Heroes' Day is on August 11, while the armed forces are honored on Armed Forces Day, August 12; December 22 is Unity Day. Christmas Day, December 25, and Boxing Day, December 26, also national holidays, round off the annual observances, with the addition of Good Friday and Easter Monday, whose dates vary.

THE PASTIMES OF THE WHITE ENCLAVES

City fare, imported by the white settlers, reflects their attempt to recreate Europe in the heart of Africa. Their enclaves not only reproduced structures reminiscent of those of their homelands, or at least standard colonial modifications of them, but their means of diversion were also derivative. They socialized with afternoon teas and barbecues and entertained themselves at home with Western music. Men in search of exercise played tennis at their whites-only clubs or joined cricket teams, and the ladies occupied themselves with lawn bowling, croquet, and the like. Their cultural nourishment consisted of European plays, and when they went to the cinema they watched mainly European (British) and American productions. When television made its appearance, its programming relied heavily on American soap operas.

Foreclosed to them during the colonial period, except in daytime as pass-carrying servants and menial workers, the cities always beckoned to Africans, who saw them as the sites of opportunities for a better life than their circumscribed villages provided. After independence in 1980, they flocked to the urban areas in search of work and the good life. In Harare the better educated ones (and the better placed ex-combatants), who constitute the elite, the so-called "chefs," moved into what had hitherto been the white, low-density residential suburb north of the railway line, as more and more whites fled to South Africa and other lands more to their liking.

Upward mobility has tended to imply (or entail) the adoption of the lifestyle ushered in by the whites, with a few nods to traditional ways: along with taking over the Europeans' residences, the new African urban elite also took over their pastimes. In some instances, city-dwellers have found substitutes for traditional village entertainment. For example, the beer-drinking *bira* performances of the villages have made the transition to the modern cities, but in a modified form as the *dandaro*. a small-scale spirit possession session that takes place in the home of the urban medium, in which hand clapping often replaces the mbira ensemble, and where the session concludes before dawn to enable the participants to get to their jobs. But for the most part, they watch television, still given to foreign programming, go to cinemas to watch mainly American movies, and patronize night clubs.

Harare residents who favor the cinema can choose from among several theaters that screen a wide spectrum of films. The city also boasts numerous night clubs where patrons can go for a *pungwe*, all-night drinking and dancing to music by some of Zimbabwe's best performers, or dance to disco music. The musical fare reflects the cosmopolitan taste of the urban Zimbabwean—local music (like Thomas Mapfumo's) mixing with music from other parts of Africa (South, West, Central), and vying with Western artists like Dolly Parton and Paul Simon.

THEATER

An estimated 100 theater groups exist in Zimbabwe, serving different demographic and cultural groups with fare peculiar to their tastes. Those serving the surviving white settler community are the best equipped, best organized, and best funded. They naturally favor plays and performances of European vintage. The Ministry of Culture also encourages various African groups to create and perform dramas that reflect Zimbabwe culture and heritage, although, again, the paucity of funds limits its effectiveness.

Residents of Harare and Bulawayo have much wider choices of theatrical entertainment than those of smaller urban centers such as Mutare and Gweru. In Harare, semiprofessional companies such as the People's Theatre, directed by Ben Sibenke, have been the most successful. Also notable are Roof Top Promotion and Mekyia Production, with performances in English and African languages that attest to the hybrid nature of Zimbabwe's official culture, and the Seven Arts Theatre. The city's Gallery Delta also offers both African and European fare. Bulawayo is home to the famous Amakhosi Theatre (a component of the Amakhosi Cultural Center), which stages African and Western productions and runs a school for training aspiring dramatists; the African dance troupe Sunduza, whose practice sessions are open to the public for a small fee; and Black Umfolosi, a group that gives *a capella* performances of English and Ndebele songs.

FASHION

Cuisine and fashion are important aspects of caring for the self, the first with regard to internal (physiological) health and stamina, and the second with regard to external (social) well-being and self-presentation as well as social acceptance. The two are interlocked by the belief that inattention to one's external condition will very likely compromise one's internal soundness, and, furthermore, that the best attire cannot lend grace to an unwashed body. We begin this discussion, therefore, with a look at external matters— the body and its adornment.

Personal Care

In his description of Mashona village life, Charles Bullock refers to their fastidiousness about personal cleanliness. He describes a scene in which young Wushe takes popcorn early in the morning to his father Mapirawana, who has gone earlier to the *dare* (meeting place). Having delivered the popcorn, "little Wushe must now go and get water; for Mapirawana will not eat without washing hands and face—only an outcast boor . . . would commit such a breach of decorum." Later on, we are presented with the scene in which Mapirawana's children sit down to eat the breakfast *sadza* (porridge) their mother places before them, and the author's observation, "I am afraid they have not had a morning bath, but hands have been washed."[6] The omission, he indicates, is extraordinary, but is mitigated by the fact that at least they are not eating with unwashed hands. Another observer provides corroboration for this fastidiousness in a description of Shona village life. It occurs in an incidental comment on the ending of a busy day in the life of teenager Tafara. "Tafara regrets not having had time to go for a swim in the river to wash herself," the writer notes. "Instead, after undressing, she pours a small bowl of water and carefully wipes her body with a rag."[7]

Tsitsi Dangarembga's description of Tambudzai's habits in *Nervous Conditions* (1989), the novel of which she is the heroine, adds substance to the impression the two foregoing examples give, especially some of the details about Tambu's domestic life in her village before her departure to live with her uncle Babamukuru at the more modern mission he runs as headmaster. The evidence is of Tambudzai's particular affection for the river, Nyamarira, where she bathed, and which she missed on moving to the mission. Her fondness for the stream is evident in her later recollection of the unrestricted access children had to it for bathing and swimming.[8] Later, recalling the occasion of her departure for the mission school, she practically rhapsodizes about the river: there would no longer be trips to Nyamarira, she recalls thinking wistfully, "Nyamarira which I loved to bathe in and watch cascade through the narrow outlet of the fall where we drew our water. Leaving this Nyamarira, my flowing, tumbling, musical playground, was difficult."[9] But she stresses that what she missed most was cavorting in the river's languid flow, certainly not the fetching of water from it in heavy pots for use at the homestead.

It has been necessary to mention the foregoing details about Shona life because colonial detractors generally betrayed a fondness for depicting the Shona as habitually filthy in their habits and habitats. It is not unusual to come upon descriptions that compare Shona people unfavorably with their Ndebele neighbors, praising the latter's cleanliness and good taste in matters of grooming and attire, but dismissing the Shona as "utterly regardless of personal cleanliness."[10] The Ndebele reputation certainly has a sound basis, for a visitor to Lobengula's court had a great deal that was complimentary to say on that score about the king, his court, and the Ndebele generally. On the other hand, there is good reason to be wary about European colonizers' descriptions of the habits and living conditions of African populations during the colonial period.

Given that the Europeans lived in secluded enclaves far removed from African settlements, and came in anything like close, intimate contact only with their domestic workers, one must be leery of their opinions on African grooming habits, especially since the habits of the domestic workers living circumscribed lives in cramped servants' quarters were not representative of normal, traditional African habits. And, in any case, Africans would not expose their most private behaviors to European audiences.

It is a matter of ironic interest that during the colonial days, African domestic workers, who had a privileged vantage point from which to observe their European employers' habits, concluded that they were generally filthy in comparison with Africans. These Africans lived in closer proximity to their European employers than Europeans did to Africans, and were well placed to be privy to Europeans' personal habits. One yet has to allow that their accounts might have been exaggerated or somewhat skewed.

What one can assert is that Africans are, as a rule, religious about their morning ablutions: the first thing an African would attend to on getting up is washing the body, the whole body, although (as has been indicated above) circumstances might dictate postponing that necessity and making do for the time being with washing only the face. In fact, one demonstrates one's good breeding by hewing to this practice even in the coldest seasons, when only the old and the infirm would resort to heating water for the morning bath without encountering some mild ribbing. Babies also were allowed the exception, of course. The foregoing generalization would of course exclude people like farmers, who must often get up before dawn to make it to their (sometimes distant) farms and put in some hard work before the day becomes oppressively hot. Such people would naturally postpone their bathing until after the sweaty work, perhaps in a stream close to their farms, or on the way home.

One study is particularly helpful in this regard, because it reveals how proper attention to differences in values from culture to culture can lead to valuable insights regarding other people's ways, while exploitative self-interest may result in inadvertent or wilful distortion of them.[11] The essay exposes the stratagems marketers of grooming products adopted in order to wean Africans from their traditional products and habits, which the marketers represented as undesirable or filthy. Thus western-style soap, pomade, hair oils, and the like were successfully marked by disparaging traditional products.

With regard to soap, long before the Lifebuoy and Lux invasion, the people of Zimbabwe, like other African peoples, had been manufacturing and using soap for centuries, exploiting locally available materials, especially palm oil. They used a ground vine with powdery leaves that has a soap-like effect, and a root they pounded and molded into cakes of soap, for washing. Furthermore, before the all too successful campaign in favor of chemical skin bleachers like Ambi seduced African women, they had groomed themselves for ages with more wholesome natural products. In Zimbabwe, the women used soil mixed with oil or animal fat to rub down their bodies, the type used depending on what was available, or what was favored, in each locality. Typically the choice soil was red, called *chivomvu* when used for this purpose, but red or yellow clay was also popular; as for the oil, it could be castor bean oil, oil from a variety of other plants, or animal fat. This traditional ointment, apart from enhancing the sheen and beauty of the skin, also served as protection against the sun and the rain. Whatever ointment the women used, though, they always used it "*along with regular washing with water.*"[12]

Bodily Marks

In addition to regularly grooming their bodies, both Shona and Ndebele groups also follow the practice of permanently scarifying themselves, or less permanently decorating their bodies for specific purposes, much like other peoples on the continent. Scarification might signify a person's belonging to a particular lineage or social class, as for example the Ndebele practice of ear piercing. They pierce their children's earlobes at about the age of ten and keep the holes open by means of wood plugs. A similar Shona practice that identifies and incorporates group members is the facial scarification called *nyora*, which indicates the ethnic group to which the bearer belongs. The "private" *nyora* was often a puberty rite, although most Shona-speaking peoples do not have elaborate puberty (initiation) rites; it was meant to enhance sexuality, and therefore only for the eyes of a husband or lover.[13] Some eastern and northeastern Shona people pierce their lips and plug the holes with nails, wire, or other materials, a practice referred to as *phuri* or *ringindi*, while others (like the Thonga) similarly pierce and plug their noses.[14]

Markings and other bodily preparations can also indicate social difference. For example, among the Ndebele only men who have achieved manhood (in the view of their peers) may wear the hair ring. "Likewise, married Ndebele women were 'allowed to wear upon the highest part of the back of the head, a peculiar ornament . . . made of oxhair, vermillion clay and fat . . . worked into spindle-shaped lengths, much resembling long thin oats, but being bulbous at one end and pointed at the other.'"[15] The Sindebele *isicolo* is a hairstyle which is peculiar to women in captivity.[16]

Clothing

Traditional clothing is simple and functional, primarily to protect the body and preserve modesty. Blankets made from bark fiber provide warmth in the cold seasons; otherwise men and women are sparing in covering their bodies. In her short story "Deciduous Gazettes" (1999) Malissa Myambo records a humorous scene in which young Zimbabwe women justify their wearing skimpy skirts by citing traditional precedent. When Irene informs her aunt, Hanna Ncube, that she and her friend Tendai are going to an afternoon session at Turtle's to listen to music—"soul, ragga [reggae], R & B"—the aunt objects to the revealing skirts the young ladies are wearing: "they were so short, so skimpy, they barely covered their underwear. Red panties were peeping out." She worried that, exposing so much of their flesh, they might be subjected to harassment from men, and they might even be arrested by the police. Her trumping argument, though, at least in her mind, was, "It's not our culture, girls." In response the young girls laughed at her and told her she was wrong on that score. They "ran to their school bags and brought out their history textbooks, pointing at illustrations of nineteenth-century Ma-Karanga and MaNdebele women, bare-breasted and clothed in two square pieces of fabric joined by a cord that barely covered their pelvises and left much of their buttocks exposed."[17] A turn-of-the-millennium observation on the new prejudices that Africans have learned in recent times perfectly describes Hanna Ncube's attitude: "In Mashonganyika village many people, especially those of grandmother's generation, had gone about scantily dressed in their *nhembe* (short leather aprons covering only the genitals) and no one had seen any shame or offence in bared breasts. But now this traditional state of innocence was unacceptable."[18]

Hanna Ncube expresses the typical modern view that has been conditioned by Western, Christian ideas about decorum and propriety, and especially uneasiness about the body. While one could be suspicious of the motives of the advocates of retaining traditional dress habits, those who argue, for example, that "a leopard skin is the ideal costume for [Africans'] bronze figures, with their fine free carriage and movement,"[19] the implications of the following opinion approving the adoption of Western habits should give one pause. It comes from a 1962 Rhodesian Ministry of Information publication:

The men have adopted the white man's national dress—shirts, trousers, coats and shoes, while the women dress exactly like European women. Cosmetics have caught on very well with almost all African women. Much money is spent on a wide range of beauty creams and lipstick. Polishing of fingernails is given much attention. Many modern young African women now have their hair stretched so that they look very much like those of European women. . . . It is evident that whatever the white man brought into this country, the African has the highest appreciation for it. What a European is, an African also wants to be.[20]

CUISINE

The staple food of the Shona people is the ubiquitous *sadza*, stiff maize meal porridge, which might serve as breakfast, lunch, or dinner. It is usually eaten with vegetables and relish and less often with meat. *Sadza* can also be made from ingredients other than maize; pea-porridge (*rutenho*) is made with beans and black-eyed peas, and *nhopi* is pumpkin porridge.

Although cattle are highly prized and beef is a favored food, the beasts are for the most part reserved for special occasions, for use as parts of bride-price, or as offerings on ritual occasions. In general, meat (especially beef, but also goat, sheep, or chicken) accompanies the meal in affluent homes or on festive occasions. Usually, when an animal is butchered, say an ox, a cow, or a goat, the butchers receive a saucepanful of blood each, a piece of liver, and a piece of the breast (if a cow) or testicles (if a bull). They boil the blood with the pieces of meat for a special dish. Wild game like crocodile and antelope is also eaten occasionally, as are locusts and white ants when they swarm. Fish is available in certain parts of the country, especially near the Kariba Dam.

The relish that goes with *sadza* can be made from a variety of vegetables, and can be seasoned with fruits and nuts and enriched with insects. For example, it could be made by boiling wild amaranthus leaves and mixing them with homemade peanut butter. Pumpkin leaves, boiled and allowed to cool, comprise another side dish. In *Nervous Conditions*, Tambudzai describes the recipe for her meat stew, which always earned high compliments. She fries goat meat gently in its own fat until it is deliciously brown, then she adds chopped onions and tomatoes to make a gravy.[21] She also makes sausages from the goat's intestines. In other recipes featuring insects, locusts are boiled in water and allowed to cool, then sun-dried for a day or two to preserve them, and stored for use bit by bit for cooking; flying ants are grilled after their wings have been removed; caterpillars are washed and boiled after their intestines have been wrung out, then dried and stored for later use, the shelf life being up to a year.[22] Additional sources of meat include mice, which the women trap and boil or grill, and birds.

Other available food items are baobab tree fruits, bananas, mangoes, and papayas. The people also cultivate grains like millet, sorghum, corn, rice, and sweet sorghum for food, although millet and sorghum are often reserved for brewing beer. Other crops are cassava (a starchy root), cowpeas, cucumbers, peanuts, sweet potatoes, pumpkins, watermelons, red peppers, pineapples, and tomatoes.

NEW HABITS FOR OLD

The impact that Western lifestyles and prejudices have had on traditional thought and habits is ubiquitously evident in Zimbabwe society. Some innocuous examples are the substitution of Western products in traditional practices, like the replacement of the traditional soil-and-fat mixture with margarine for anointing or "smearing" the body.[23] The loss of knowledge, expertise, or technology involved is not so innocuous, of course. The technology and practice of mixing and using red or yellow soil and some sort of oil as part of daily hygiene have virtually disappeared. Fortunately, the use of plants like *ruredzo* and *chitupatupa* in soap-making has persisted and is still popular in some rural areas.

More troubling is the modern Zimbabwean's tendency to denigrate traits that set Africans apart from Europeans. One such trait is skin color. Several African writers have had a great deal to say against the industry that has developed, and continues to thrive, on the successful indoctrination of Africans, especially African women, into believing that a lighter skin is preferable to a darker one. In "Deciduous Gazettes" Hanna Ncube's friends express their sympathy for her, and their solidarity with her against her rival for her husband's affection, by remarking on the other woman's darker skin: "*Akashata! Maiwe!* She's so dark, *kana pasi pebodo pari mani!*" [Ugly! My! . . . The bottom of the pot is better than her]. Ncube is more sensitive in this regard than her friends: "Why do my people still do this," she wonders, "isn't it bad enough that whites censure our colour? Now we too must do the same thing. Or perhaps we always did it."[24]

Furthermore, urbanization, necessitated by the imperative of finding gainful employment, has drastically reduced the influence of the family and the community in the affairs of individuals. Modern Zimbabweans do not necessarily see the development as regrettable, for escape to the urban setting is, to many, a shedding of traditional fetters. For example, in *Shadows*, Chanjerai Hove gives as one of Johana's father's reasons for leaving his village for Gotami's land and entering into tutelage to the white settlers the wish to escape his obligations to the traditional Hutu chief. On his own farm, given to him by the white authorities, he will be free of the headman and the chief; he will be free to approach the ancestors, "not through the headman or the chief," but directly.[25]

But that freedom carries a price. In the novel it is no less than the deaths of Johana's father, his sons, and Johana. In real life, urban dwellers are deprived of the teachings the old impart to the young about how to behave properly, or how to respect others, especially the elders. In the cities, a new structure has developed to replace the old one based on age, kinship, and hereditary status. At the apex are the well-educated and westernized professionals: lawyers, doctors, and bureaucrats, the "chefs," who constitute a middle class and live in the old white suburbs. They marry their own kind— well-educated, westernized women—and often speak English rather than

Shona or Ndebele at home. Because they ordinarily have household servants, their children do not learn the responsibility of having to do household chores or of helping their elders with errands.

One strategy for rectifying the deprivation is for parents to send their children to live in the villages for a time so they can have access to the wisdom of those who have remained within the tradition. As for the adults, they resort to a variety of urban social outlets as replacement for the communal, age-based groups: "Women join women's clubs in which they give each other help in running their homes. Many men join soccer clubs and some join burial societies which, along with giving members a proper funeral when the time comes, also provide social activities. Churches, youth clubs, charitable organizations, and workers' unions all help to bridge the gap from the old life to the new."[26] These expedients may help, but it is difficult to think that any association in the impersonal city can quite measure up to the traditional bond predicated on the trust and security of shared ancestry and ancestral watchfulness.

NOTES

1. Solomon M. Mutswairo, *Mapondera, Soldier of Zimbabwe* (Washington, DC: Three Continents Press, 1978), 45.
2. Ibid.
3. Michael Gelfand, *Shona Religion, with Special Reference to the Makorekore* (Cape Town, Wynberg, and Johannesburg: Juta & Co., 1962), 13–15.
4. Charles Bullock, *The Mashona (The Indigenous Natives of S. Rhodesia)* (1928; reprint, Westport, CT: Negro Universities Press, 1970), 245.
5. Ibid., 247.
6. Bullock, 246–47.
7. Patricia Cheney, *The Land and People of Zimbabwe* (New York: J. B. Lippincott, 1990), 206.
8. Tsitsi Dangarembga, *Nervous Conditions* (Seattle, WA: Seal Press, 1989), 3.
9. Ibid., 59.
10. Timothy Burke, *Lifebuoy Men, Lux Women: Commodification, Consumption, and Cleanliness in Modern Zimbabwe* (Durham: Duke University Press, 1996), 19.
11. Ibid.
12. Ibid., 24; italics added.
13. John S. Mbiti, *African Religions and Philosophy* (New York: Praeger, 1969), 28.
14. Ibid., 26.
15. Ibid., 27–28.
16. Bullock, 248.
17. Malissa Tandiwe Myambo, "Deciduous Gazettes," in *Opening Spaces: An Anthology of Contemporary African Women's Writing*, ed. Yvonne Vera (Oxford: Heinemann, 1999), 14.

18. Burke, 43.

19. Ibid., 22.

20. Quoted in ibid., 149–50.

21. Dangarembga, 39.

22. Cheney, 205.

23. Burke, 162–63.

24. Myambo, 16.

25. Chanjerai Hove, *Shadows* (Oxford: Heinemann, 1991), 42.

26. Cheney, 202.

6

Gender Roles, Marriage, and Family

CLARIFYING WOMEN'S STATUS

THE STATUS AND ROLE OF WOMEN are among the least understood aspects of African traditional social organization, in part because there are no contemporary written studies of African societies before the arrival of Europeans. Consequently, the earliest records are those of the earliest European visitors, who based what they wrote on what they observed as outsiders. Moreover, many of these Europeans were either missionaries or agents of European governments or commercial companies; they could not always tell the difference between appearance and reality, between formal role playing and actual living. Furthermore, since the early European presence was overwhelmingly male, interactions, such as they were, were between European and African men. Consequently, if, despite the demands of propriety and delicacy, these European men had been inclined to probe into matters concerning African women and their relationships with their men, their African informers could have been expected to reveal little, in keeping with their own notions of propriety.

The foregoing is not to say that the early records are entirely useless. Perceptive European observers have left us with detailed descriptions of ceremonies, performances, and the like, including such things as the rituals pertaining to betrothal and marriage, the installation of chiefs, funerals, and so forth. In some instances also, when these observers have asked about the significance of certain ceremonies their informants have been forthcoming, especially as long as ritual secrets were not involved. At other times, of course, European observers have resorted to their own interpretations, based on their Western values.

More recent studies and exposés of traditional African social institutions, processes, and relationships, especially by Africans, have gone a long way in revealing the truths about them and in correcting many distortions, but some misunderstandings and misconceptions persist. In some cases, unfortunately, the Africans who have undertaken studies and descriptions of traditional African life have tended to compound the problem; having been educated in Western schools and socialized into Western values, they have approached their subject with the same Western prejudices and preconceptions as their European mentors.

A scholar discussing the status of women in Zimbabwe recently pronounced them subordinate to men, in accord with a pattern typical of all patriarchal societies. Women's inferior status was attributed to several factors: the gift men present to the parents of their brides as part of the marriage arrangement (*lobola*); marriage systems whereby women leave their homes and become part of their husbands' families; men's ownership and control of land and other means of production; limited legal rights for women; and their minimal participation in political and religious institutions.[1] With particular reference to Shona women, another scholar, basing the analysis on the evidence Tsitsi Dangarembga (a Shona woman) provides in her novel *Nervous Conditions* (1989), argues that they are at the mercy of the authoritative men in their family, and cites the "almost divine power that [Tambu's] uncle holds over the women in the family," which, it is suggested, makes Nyasha, Tambu's cousin, "largely disgusted with the status of the women in the family."[2]

Another form of imposition to which Zimbabwe women are said to be subject is the requirement that they wait on the men in their families practically all day, and otherwise perform all the chores at home and on the farm, while the men sit in the *dare* drinking beer and smoking. An observer comments as follows on the relationship between eighteen-year-old Tafara and her fifteen-year-old brother Tichagwa:

> [S]he knows he won't help her. At present he is enjoying his status as an adolescent male. Although Tichagwa does not yet have the privileges of a grown man, Tafara is no longer permitted to boss him around, and each night she brings him his food as he sits with the adult men in the *dare*.[3]

Another commentator reports that even at social functions involving dancing, matronly women may attend but as a rule cannot join in the dance, unless they have mastered a special step; rather, they make themselves useful by joining in providing the music.[4]

In opposition to the impression the foregoing leaves us with regard to the place of women in Zimbabwe society, another Shona woman quotes a Tonga woman as saying that "women held a privileged position among the Tonga because it was a matria[r]chal society. Land and other possessions were inherited through the female line; when a chief died, for instance, the chieftainship was passed down to his sister's son."[5] And one would be wrong to conclude from her observation that esteem for women was limited to matrilocal groups, in which husbands reside with their wives' families, and matrilineal groups. With regard to the assignment of duties, for example, one can demonstrate that, appearances to the contrary notwithstanding, some equity does exist in what is expected of both genders.

GENDER DIVISION OF LABOR

In traditional Zimbabwe society, and in those across Africa as a whole, men and women had well-defined roles and obligations that were specific and exclusive to their respective genders. The division of labor was such that the domestic sphere, on the one hand, belonged to the woman, and there her authority was unchallenged; the public domain, on the other hand, belonged to the man, and neither arena was regarded as superior to the other. The woman had the sole responsibility of distributing food and otherwise managing household affairs. Women also did some work outside the home, to be sure. For example, they did most of the lighter farm work, like planting and weeding, while the heavier work—felling trees and clearing the land—fell to the men. Women also participated in the harvesting, in addition to keeping their own gardens, the produce of which they disposed of as they pleased. On the other hand, men did all the heavy work around the home, for example, building the walls for the huts. Women's employment on the farm did not constitute an excessive and unfair burden to them, and men did not sit around while the women worked. The following observation on this subject, made by a Westerner in the 1920s, deserves to be quoted at length:

> [Women] do not do all the work, as is sometimes supposed. Here is a division of labour which ought to obtain if custom is kept. . . .
>
> Husband cuts the poles, and builds and thatches the hut, taking care to leave *zwipanda* [wooden pegs] in the walls, on which things may be hung; he builds also the *bakwa* [wood storage area] for the firewood.
>
> He makes the bark sacks and the *baskets—dengu, dengwana, shandiro, hwanda (tswanda), misero, chisergwana, gombo,* etc. He makes the reed sleeping-mat and the pillow of wood. He makes hoe-handles, axe-shafts and bow; also wooden plates, spoons and porridge sticks.

He tans wife's skins, *shashiko* or *chitore* and *nhembe*; as well as his own (*nere, mapa, newe maringa* and *kahanda*).

He makes the drum for the dance and tunes it. He used to make *mnondo*, the two-edged dagger . . . .

The man should milk, and the youths herd the cattle. Husband should do all the heavy work in the lands. He breaks the new ground and ploughs up the old, but in this he is generally helped by the co-operation of neighbours attracted by a prospect of beer. He cannot stump, so he cuts down the branches of trees, and burns them at the roots; and again cuts down the new shoots, so that the tree may die and the ashes form a fertiliser.

He reaps, helped by his wife; and even so, he threshes.

He hunts, and traps fish with *matuwu*, the basket trap he makes. He joins other men in the hunt with the dogs and the net, and he may make a game-pit or a garden trap. He makes the game-net *mambure*, and the *misungo, mabote* and *mikuni* staves for it. Also the smaller-meshed net for guinea-fowl. He is the butcher and skinner.[6]

As for the woman:

Wife treads the *daga* [puddles], plaisters [*sic*] the walls, smears the floor of the hut, and builds inside it *chitukuriro*, a raised place not too near the fire-place where her husband can sit. *Chikuwa* and *chigadzikiro* where the pots may stand, and *chibeso* the clay hearth where *mabfiwa* the three hearth stones are placed, are all built by her.

She makes the jugs and pots—*chirongo* for water, *gate* for beer or water; *fuko, mbidziro* and *nyengero* for beer; *shambakodzi*, the big cooking pot and *hadhlana* or *mbiya* for savouries. She has no potter's wheel and the moulding, drying, decorating and burning take a week to complete.

Wife cuts *godhla* which is soft grass to sleep on. She threads beads, and she smears *mbereko* in which she carries baby. Once she used to make garments from bark—*mapfunu na makumbu e gudza*.

The woman has nothing to do with cattle, or should not have. She cooks the food and draws water.

She helps to prepare the soil, and weeds the lands after planting. The beer she brews draws young men who will probably do more work than her husband. She also has her own land to look after.

She helps her husband to reap and to thresh. She stamps mealies and so gets fine arms and shoulders. She winnows, and she *guwa's* (husks corn); and a good wife will not throw away the inner husk she so separates, but mix it with meal and make porridge [*sic*].

She grinds the meal.

She also catches white ants and caterpillars; and poisons fish with *mukone, mhandwe, chitupatupa* and *zhombgwe,* and cuts them open very quickly to clean them. She joins with other women in getting fish, by forcing the water up with leafy branches from a nearly dry pool, and leaving the fish high and dry.

She seeks edible fungi, and *miriwo* which are wild herbs for the savoury.

"A fair division of labour?" he asks, and responds, "It was not so very unfair as Europeans once thought, but times and habits are changing now."[7]

WOMEN'S ATTITUDE TOWARD MARRIAGE AND MOTHERHOOD

The attribution of Zimbabwe women's supposedly inferior status to marriage and its associated conditions would logically suggest that the women would be ill disposed to the institution, and by extension to motherhood, and even to the whole notion of domesticity (meaning here the condition of being close to the hearth). The opposite is oftentimes true. Whereas the modern European woman might take offense at the suggestion that a woman's place is in the home, the traditional African woman would see nothing objectionable in it. In addition, the traditional Zimbabwe woman looks forward to wifehood and motherhood; being unmarried after attaining the age of marriage is a cause for anxiety and embarrassment for the woman and her family, and failure to bear children after marriage is reason for worry for all concerned, triggering measures to find some remedy for the problem.

Marriage confers specific benefits on women. Women consolidate their domestic position and social status through marriage and reproduction, especially the bearing of male children. And, as with the men, as they advance in age their views command increasing attention in family deliberations and decision making, their influence being greatest when they become grandmothers. With age, also, they gain attentive hearing in communal discussions, even though they do not participate formally in group councils. Women's relative lack of public visibility in comparison with men belies the fact that behind the scenes they often call the shots.

THE TRADITIONAL FAMILY: LOCALITY AND LINEALITY

Attempts to make any generally applicable deduction about the status of Zimbabwe women on the basis of whether a woman moves into her husband's home on marriage or vice versa would be futile, if only because there is no uniformity in the matter. In general, the Shona follow a patrilineal (descent through males) kinship system and practice virilocality, wives relocating is their husbands' groups. Under patriliny, the lines of descent and authority are traced through fathers: a man and his brothers, their children, and their sons' children are counted as members of the same descent group. Fathers, and male heads of the family especially, are owed respect and obedience as the immediate representatives of the lineage or clan (often identified by a totem). Children tend to view fathers and male family heads as emotionally distant disciplinary authorities, whatever the degree of affection they may have for each other. A wife, at the time of her marriage, exchanges the authority of her father for that of her husband, and usually a wife is gradually absorbed into her husband's patrilineal descent group. Women are also counted as members of their patrilineal descent groups, but their children will belong to their father's rather than their mother's kinship groups. Matrilineal links are thus of secondary importance in the social scheme of a patrilineal society.

In matrilocal and matrilineal groups like the Tonga, a man moves in with his wife's family on marriage; if he subsequently marries another wife, he moves in with the new wife for a while, and thereafter divides his time between the wives' homes. Inheritance of land and other possession passes through the women, including chieftaincy titles, which pass from a dead chief to his sister's son.

LOBOLA AND THE STATUS OF WOMEN

The *lobola* (bride-price) has become, for many scholars, an index of the diminished status of the traditional African woman, because they see it as proof that she is simply a commodity men exchange among themselves for their own benefit. It has served as an excuse for even African women to refer to marriage as the sale and purchase of women by men. The Nigerian author Buchi Emecheta, for example, is fond of writing about marriage as the purchase of wives.[8] The translation of the applicable African word into English alternatively as "bride-price" and "bride wealth" has reinforced and perpetuated the misrepresentation, the first with its unfortunate connotation of a market transaction, and the second with its misleading suggestion that the amounts involved are substantial. A comprehensive look at marriage in traditional Zimbabwe societies will help to clarify the matter.

Lobola (lobolo, ukulobola) or *roora* is an arrangement by which the bride's family group receives livestock, other goods, and (more recently) cash or opportunities to earn cash as a compensation for the loss of their daughter's productivity. A father explains his request for *lobola* for his daughter Tafara with the argument that she is his eldest daughter and an invaluable help to her mother when he is away. The mother therefore is the one who will suffer the most hardship after Tafara's marriage.[9] The payment thus represents an alternative to the matrilocal *ku garira* system of marriage (see below), in which the man is incorporated into the woman's family. It also bonds the two families and binds the husband to treat his wife well.

Furthermore, in patrilineal Shona marriages, the children that result are traditionally legitimized by the exchange of *roora*. According to a pertinent saying, "The children are where the cattle are not,"[10] meaning that the home from which cattle are transferred to another as *lobola* is the one that keeps the children of the marriage. An indication that it is not a purchase payment is the fact that "the cognomen of the wife remains unchanged on marriage. A Heart remains a Heart when she marries a Pool, and spirit Hearts still control the mainsprings of her life; nor do they altogether relegate her children to the spirit Pools of their father."[11] Another source notes, "One thing at least is certain, and that is that the Native does not associate with the payment of *lobola* the notions that we associate with the usual word purchase."[12]

As for the amounts involved, traditionally, what was exchanged was never intended to represent the actual value of the woman, but a symbolic amount, a token. The involvement of money these days is a response to the substitution of a monetized economy for what prevailed traditionally and to an increasing dissolution of extended family ties, and it has entailed the incorporation of the crass associations of lucre. Instead of cooperative unions between two extended families, marriages, even in rural areas, have become arrangements between the groom and the bride's father mainly or exclusively, thus cheapening the institution and the people involved (see later discussion of "arranged" marriages). But the evidence of Chenjerai Hove's novel *Bones* (1988), a work that is pro-feminist in tone and concept and quite critical of men, is that mothers are sometimes implicated in attempts to secure some material gain from the marriage of their daughters. In the novel, adolescent Janifa's mother connives with Chisaga, a much older man, to facilitate his raping her, and lies to protect him from police investigators.[13] Also, in disregard of Janifa's pains resulting from the damage Chisaga did to her, she wants her to marry the man in any case, "so that cattle can come to her house while she still has good teeth to eat them."[14] Janifa therefore embarks on a painful trek to her mother's home, saying, "I have to walk on until I can see my mother. I want to see her so that I can spit in her face before I leave her."[15]

CONSTANCY OF INTEREST IN MARRIED DAUGHTERS

The extent to which the place a woman occupies in her family changes on her marriage is a good indication of her esteem in it. In market transactions a seller properly loses all interest in an article once he has sold it. In Shona society, however, a woman does not forfeit the interest of her own family in her welfare when she moves into her marital home. On the contrary, she retains her connection with the former, which continues to offer her its protection, and a refuge if necessary—if the marriage situation becomes abusive, or if she is divorced or widowed. Practical demonstrations of the connection may take the form of exchanging mutual help during harvests and festive occasions, and sharing farm products at harvest and food during feasts. At times, they take more significant guises. One example is the case of Mai Hilda, who had suffered three miscarriages and had failed to carry any pregnancy to term. Her sister intervened by sending her own two-year-old daughter, also named Hilda, to live with Mai Hilda. The intervention was considered necessary because of the importance Shona people, including Shona women, attach to childbearing and motherhood. A married woman looks forward to the delivery of her first baby, after which event she will be known in the community as the Mother of So and So, the preferred form of address among married women. A married woman without a child is therefore always reminded of her misfortune, as are members of her family and others who interact with her. Mai Hilda's sister accordingly acted "to spare her the shame of not being called by a child's name."[16]

The family comes to the rescue of a woman in Mai Hilda's predicament in other ways, for example, offering another woman from the family to the husband to bear children for him, and thus become another wife to him. The arrangement defuses any resentment he might otherwise harbor against his wife. In cases in which the failure to bear a child is not attributable to any disability on the woman's part but rather to her husband's inadequacy, the woman's family intervenes in a different manner. Her aunt or a senior female relative will advise her to permit a male relative of the husband, a brother or cousin, to "enter her bedroom" and help her to conceive. The matter will be kept secret, known only to select elders in the family. The woman's desire for children will be fulfilled, and all offspring from the arrangement will be acknowledged as her husband's.

With regard to circumstances in which family members act to save the face of a woman who cannot have children, one can legitimately argue that such a woman's predicament results from patriarchal imposition of expectations, but such an argument serves only to construe women as feckless, passive objects.

PROTECTING WOMEN IN LABOR

A married woman's natal family demonstrates its continued interest in her welfare even after her marriage in another way, also connected with childbearing. According to tradition, when a woman in her first pregnancy enters into labor, she is required, in order to secure a safe and easy delivery, to confess to her attendants if she has engaged in any extramarital affairs. Because of the tradition's potential for seriously marring relations between husbands and indiscreet wives, a woman usually returns to her parents' home for her first delivery, secure in the knowledge that any damaging confession she makes will be kept from her husband and his family.

In the case of matrilocal societies, of course, the question of married wives losing or retaining the support of their families would not arise.

"FORCED MARRIAGE"

In certain Shona subgroups, the prospective groom might join the bride's family even before the birth of his future bride. That means, of course, that in such cases the marriage is arranged without the bride's consent. The absence of consultation with the bride, and of her consent, has prompted some scholars to describe such an arrangement as a "forced marriage." The logic of such a characterization is unassailable from a Western perspective, but not necessarily so from the point of view of Africans socialized into accepting the good offices of older relatives who, they are convinced, have their best interests at heart. As an example, when Lydia, a Tonga community health worker, explained that she had married a disabled man much older than herself because he had approached her father, and between them the two men had settled the matter, her westernized auditor concluded, "So it was a forced marriage." But Lydia was emphatic in her objection: "Oh no," she laughed, and then went on to endorse the arrangement and express her appreciation of her husband. "I knew my husband and his family before I married him," she said. "Apart from his crippled leg, there is nothing wrong with him. He really is a good man. . . . Believe me, he has never laid his hands on me. He still lives with me in the family compound and he has not taken another wife after me."[17]

WIFE INHERITANCE

Another marriage-related traditional practice that Western (and westernized) observers take as evidence of the devaluation and exploitation of women is wife inheritance. According to this practice, which is widespread in Africa, a widowed woman may be taken in marriage by a surviving (usually younger) male relative of her husband. The real reason is the desire to provide security for the widow, now bereft of her source of support, and her children. But the institution has been subjected to gross misinterpretation, most famously in Senegalese Mariama Bâ's celebrated novel *So Long a Letter*

(1981). In this view, it is nothing more than a ruse men devised to deprive women of their just inheritance, and to secure wives effortlessly and on the cheap into the bargain. But even in that work the author establishes that whereas a male relative of the deceased husband may ask the woman to become his wife, she is by no means obliged to consent. Thus Ramatoulaye spurns the hand Tamsir, her dead husband Modou's brother, extends in marriage.[18]

Sekai Nzenza-Shand's *Songs to an African Sunset* offers a good illustration of how the institution works among the Shona. At the ceremony two years after Charles's death, in which his wife Rudo is expected to end her mourning period and select a husband from among his younger male siblings, she refuses to accept any of the proffered hands. In the end, she presents the symbolic bowl of water to Kumbi, her ten-year-old son, signifying to all present that he is her choice. For the benefit of anyone who might misconstrue this, a witness explains, "Eh, guys, don't get so excited. This is only a ceremony. All it means is that Mai Kumbi [Kumbi's mother] is now a free woman."[19] Incidentally, years earlier, when Charles's mother was in Rudo's situation, she too had rejected all suitors and chosen her oldest son as her inheritor.

POLYGAMY

The practice of polygamy—having more than one spouse—in traditional African societies has always intrigued Western observers, who understand marriage to be an exclusive relationship between a loving couple, and consider any intimacy by one of the partners with another person besides the spouse as a betrayal, an infidelity. The instances of such intimacy, in their normal experience, are usually secretive. They therefore find it difficult to understand a system that permits a person to formally and openly marry several partners. Understandably, because it is usually the man who may marry several wives and not the other way round, the system appears unfair to women, and thus to be another indication of the inferior status of women in the society. Briefly, polygamy was sustained by socioeconomic factors that made it more attractive to men and women alike than monogamy. Furthermore, although most (but not all) modern African women are critical of it, traditional women were quite comfortable with it in the cultural context that sustained it. That is the explanation for such laments as the following that one hears from women who remember the old days: "Oh, polygamy! What does it offer women these days except poverty? . . . In the old days, you enjoyed the support of other wives, mothers-in-law and aunts. If your husband favored one wife over the others, you could complain to the village elders. Not any more."[20]

One misconception about polygamy is that it was a concession to men's promiscuous tendencies. In fact, the opposite is true, for Shona society is typical in abhorring such excesses. In fact, although polygamy was the norm in the society, in practice monogamy was quite prevalent, the typical family comprising a man, his wife, and their children, although that unit constituted part of an extended family. Today, the law proscribes polygamy, but the practice has not died.

WOMEN'S INVOLVEMENT IN SOCIETY

Women play prominent roles in social functions, both in those that involve women only and in those in which both genders participate. In the distant past, the Monomotapa kingdom had women warriors, and the women's army had the final say in electing the king.[21] The story of Ambuya Nehanda (see Chapter 1) and her central role in fomenting the first *chimurenga* is a hallowed part of Zimbabwe history, and today female mediums and herbal doctors keep her heritage alive.

A curious provision for responding to an ancestor-induced illness offers an important indication of Shona traditional regard for women. Sometimes, when a young child is ill, a medium might reveal that the illness is a signal from the child's grandfather that he wants some beer. The child's father must then arrange for some women to brew beer, three pots of which he presents to the ancestral spirits: one to the father of the grandfather who made the request, one to the grandfather himself, and one to the grandfather's wife.[22] The point here is that the grandfather's wife is not left out of the sacrifice.

Also, customarily the duty of brewing beer for ritual purposes is reserved for women, just as the dancing of the *mafuwe* at the annual *marenje* ceremony is their exclusive preserve. One can interpret the assignment of these duties to women as instances of women's exploitation, or one can see them as acknowledgment of women's special powers and of the necessity of making space for women's involvement.

A GENDER-SENSITIVE SOCIETY

It sometimes happens that the spirit of a dead person returns to plague members of a family that wronged him during his lifetime, or that was somehow responsible for his death. The spirit, or *ngozi*, might demand a bride from the offending family if they wish to be left in peace. In one such instance, Maria's family sent her to Chiutzi's family for atonement, because their men had had a hand in his death. The older women in Maria's family enthusiastically endorsed the arrangement, provoking Sydney, a male relative, to chastise them for sacrificing Maria for the offense of men, who remained free to live their lives as they chose. "It is not fair. We must change these traditions," he said.[23] This story testifies to an enlightened gender sensitivity on the part of one man, but more impressive are institutionalized processes through which wronged or powerless women can obtain redress. The first is the institution of *bopoto*, and the second is a ritual an erring son must perform to appease his wronged mother, or her spirit if she is dead.

BOPOTO

Bopoto is a mechanism built into traditional Shona social customs to safeguard the interests of women, especially those of women in weak positions, against powerful authority figures. The aggrieved woman encamps outside the home of the person against whom she has a grievance and declaims loudly, thus drawing a crowd. Usually the community's elders would come to the scene and persuade the woman to present her case in a calm manner. Having heard her, they would arrange for a solution that would ensure the return of peace and tranquility. Women resort to *bopoto* only when they are up against powerful figures, like clan patriarchs, and have sought all other means to resolve the problem but failed. It is not a process for settling simple squabbles or casual disagreements.[24]

ATONEMENT AND PURIFICATION

Shona society mandates the remedy of purification for any man who has committed a serious offense against his mother. Mothers "are traditionally regarded as sacred in Shona culture. You can easily get away with assaulting your father but never your mother. If you have committed a crime against your mother, you must prove that you are genuinely sorry by performing specified purifying rituals."[25] The atonement is more urgent when the mother dies before the son can seek forgiveness. Failure to atone as prescribed is a guarantee of serious misfortune for the offender in the future.

The man concerned covers himself with ashes and goes around the village wearing sackcloth. As he makes his rounds, he sits by rubbish heaps, where people throw more ashes at him, as well as pebbles and sticks. They jeer at him and berate him for daring to insult his mother. Someone might make a necklace out of corn husks and place it around his neck, and another might then give him cold porridge to eat with salt water. Having thus abused him, the people then give him sorghum or maize, which he puts in a sack he carries over his shoulders. He continues the routine until he has collected ten buckets of sorghum and three buckets of maize. For two days following, he performs the woman's job of grinding the sorghum, accepting no help from anyone. He prepares three drums of beer from the ground sorghum, and then informs the elders of his community that he is ready for the final cleansing ceremony. The entire village attends the event, which includes the killing of an ox that the people assembled eat without salt. All that done, the offending son then publicly asks his mother's spirit for forgiveness.[26]

THE DISRUPTIVE EFFECTS OF THE EUROPEAN PRESENCE

Without a doubt, women are subject to certain disadvantages in modern Zimbabwe vis-à-vis men, but this does not reflect the way things have always been. Traditional social arrangements took account of women's interests in communal affairs and provided for their full participation on a par with men, although in most cases the genders operated as exclusive groups with discrete functions. The actions of the earliest Europeans to penetrate the continent and impose their will are largely responsible for many of the disadvantages women face today in comparison to men in African societies. For example, the first Europeans, who as a rule were men, brought their chauvinistic Victorian prejudices with them and interacted only with local men, paying scant attention to the presence or interests of women. Moreover, in the process of forcefully appropriating African lands and maneuvering the deprived people into the role of cheap hired labor, the white settlers drastically distorted the time-honored relationship between men and women, and exacerbated the resulting inequities by passing laws and regulations that further disadvantaged women in relation to men.

In traditional Shona society it was not unusual for a woman to own land in her own right. In matrilineal, matrilocal societies inheritance passed through them, and, in any case, women usually had full control of plots of land near the homestead, which they farmed, and the produce of which was theirs to use as they saw fit. Their contribution to the family's resources from these plots was a source of pride and self-esteem. The white settlers appropriated most of the good land, crowding the indigenous people into cramped, sterile enclaves. When they allocated plots to Africans, these went to the men, and since women could not own farms they were also excluded from the little financial aid available to African farmers and from access to the technological help available to native farmers. Because traditionally women were able to augment the family's resources with what they produced on their plots, the loss of these plots caused some diminution in their self-respect and the respect they enjoyed within the home.

The settlers' policies and regulations not only curtailed men's farming abilities, but also their ability to hunt, and the number of livestock they could keep and graze. Migrant labor policies and the imposition of hut taxes and the like, even though they affected only the men directly, caused enormous hardship for the women also. As the men were forced to go to labor camps, at times for upwards of three years at a time, the women left behind had to look after the families and homesteads on their own, sometimes with no remittances coming from their absent husbands for the duration. Even when the men farmed close to home, the requirement that they produce cash crops rather than food crops did little to ease the women's predicament, since these were crops that children cannot eat.

When agricultural production declined toward the end of the colonial period, many women followed their husbands to the cities, sharing their subsistence on meager wages. Comparing the reduced circumstances women had to endure with the lifestyle they enjoyed before the arrival of the whites, a woman lamented, "It is very un-African and dehumanizing to be so dependent that one has to ask for money for salt from a husband."[27]

SOCIAL RAMIFICATIONS OF THE NEW ECONOMY

The new economy, which drastically reduced, and sometimes eliminated, men's capacity to raise cattle, worked to women's disadvantage also, for example in connection with marriage transactions. Traditionally the prospective groom gave some head of cattle to the bride's family as a gesture of appreciation for their part in raising the woman and as a token of his esteem for his prospective bride. The reduction or elimination of men's cattle holdings meant that they could no longer make the gesture, or could not make it adequately. The necessary resort to money as a substitute has resulted in making the transaction seem like the exchange of a commodity, thus commodifying the woman and diminishing her prestige.

COLONIAL ERA MODIFICATIONS CONCERNING MARRIAGE

Colonial statutes recognized registered traditional marriages in which the husband had paid the *lobola* to the bride's family, and also unregistered marriages in which only part of the *lobola* had been paid. In contrast to traditional Shona and Ndebele practice, whereby estranged couples lived apart but continued to be formally married, the colonial regime permitted divorce in both traditional and civil marriages; in unregistered marriages an agreement between the men of both households involved sufficed, whereas in registered marriages the action of a village court was required.

With regard to property rights, colonial law recognized the woman's right to own property, but her husband was entitled to her income, which was often paid directly to him and was heavily taxed. In the event of divorce, the law entitled her to one year's support from her husband (if the husband was employed in the public sector); if she became widowed, she was entitled to a year's support from her husband's family. In either case, she was entitled to the custody of all children below the age of seven. Older children belonged to the husband or his family. A widowed woman who chose not to marry a male relative of her dead husband returned to her family's home as an independent adult; she was entitled to take with her, her clothes, cooking utensils, and whatever she might have accumulated from her profession. She also remained entitled to the "mother's cow," her share of the *lobola* paid for her daughters.

THE WEAKENED FAMILY

The new social arrangements have weakened the family and in effect reduced women's quality of life. The dispersal and fragmentation of the traditional family have cost grandmothers the prestige they used to enjoy, because its basis (oversight of the family young) is gone. Furthermore, the modern school, supposedly a harbinger of all good things imaginable, has also affected the traditional woman's position negatively. Free primary education enticed older children away from their traditional role of caring for their younger siblings and generally helping around the home. Elderly women, who in the past could count on the older children to help them, must now employ paid household help. And grandmothers, who in the past derived a measure of importance and a sense of purpose from looking after their grandchildren, can no longer play that role, because their children move to the cities with the grandchildren and send them to kindergartens and day-care centers.

AFRICAN WOMEN IN THE COLONIAL URBAN SETTING

Most African women in colonial urban settings fell into two broad categories: traditional urban dwellers, that is, women who remained traditional in all particulars but resided in, or at the margins of, Western (or westernized) urban society; and westernized African women whose lives were closely associated with colonial institutions, including the Christian missions. The first category was made up substantially of the dependents of men who were employed in the urban areas, or those who migrated there in search of menial jobs or as prostitutes. They are of some interest, among other reasons, for the dilemma they caused the white administration, which was never quite sure how to control them, and for the modest (but yet meaningful) way they found to confound the authorities.

Typically, the white society worked much more closely with African men than with the women. Traditionally, women stayed close to their communities, while men were freer to venture, as colonial policy indeed induced them to, into the urban areas for wage employment. They therefore supplied the domestic help (as cooks, washer-men, and the like) in the white households. The presence of so many African men in and near white dwellings caused the usual anxieties in colonial circles; it gave rise to the fear among the settlers of the "black peril" constituted by supposedly oversexed black men within white homes.[28] That was one of the reasons for the pass laws, according to which any African man entering the city had to carry a pass that would certify that he was employed by a white family and specify his employment.

African women were for long exempt from such laws. The reason was not that the colonizers intended to confer preferential treatment on them; indeed, it was the opposite, for the white people considered them to be of little consequence. Even so, some in the colonial circle thought it prudent to impose the same conditions on African women, for their presence in the cities posed its own problem, for example, the resort by many of them to prostitution. Even though some colonial officials patronized the prostitutes, they nevertheless disliked the fact that they were outside official control. In this particular regard the desires of the colonizers and those of African male authorities coincided, since as early as 1900 African officials had pleaded with the Native Department to enforce the pertinent customary laws to discourage African women from migrating to the cities.

From the 1920s through the 1940s the authorities were pestered with repeated demands that women be included in the pass laws' provisions. They resisted the pressure until the late 1970s, mainly because they were aware that when, a while earlier, South Africa attempted to bring South African women under its pass laws it encountered serious trouble, and they wanted to avoid a similar experience. In any case, throughout the colonial era, Rhodesian law accorded the African woman, regardless of education, wealth, or marital status, only the legal status of a child. Accordingly, the authorities considered her mobility and freedom of action already sufficiently restricted. When every African came under the pass laws after UDI (1965), African women subversively clung to their earlier "privilege," to the discomfiture of the authorities. According to a firsthand account, whenever an African woman was asked to produce her pass, she responded, "How can you ask me for a *chitupa*, am I a man?"[29]

THE CLIENTS OF COLONIALISM

The second category of Zimbabwe women figured prominently in the colonial scheme as agents of socialization and change. From about the end of

World War II, the white settlers began to pay increasing attention to devising solutions to certain troubling developments within the colony that had been gathering pace since the turn of the century, including the "black peril." The white settlers' Victorian sensibilities had never been comfortable with the idea of men as domestic workers, and, furthermore, they would rather have African men working in the primary industries than in Europeans' kitchens. The obvious solution was to co-opt African women and impress them into domestic service. Whites were not displeased, therefore, to see increasing numbers of African women fleeing their communities and the authority of their male relatives (including husbands) for the freedom of the cities, where they were a welcome substitute for African men in domestic positions. The Christian missions for their part saw in the urban female African population an opportunity for proselytizing and civilizing, and for serving the settler society by providing the requisite training for the female domestic workers it desired. They accordingly set up training institutions where these women learned laundry and other domestic chores. The missionaries also intended the institutions as breeding grounds for "proper" Christian wives for their male preachers and converts. When they undertook this last function the missionaries effectively emasculated African patriarchs, for by assuming the role of supplying wives to their African men and contracting marriages, they usurped "one of the most fundamental forms of power held by elder kin in Shona and Ndebele society alike."[30]

CLEANING UP THE AFRICANS

One way in which the missionaries used African women in their civilizing mission was to enlist them as agents in the attempt to change African habits, especially their notions of hygiene. Accordingly, they trained African women as "Jeanes teachers" and later posted them to different locations to teach domestic subjects and conduct "home demonstrations." The teachers operated, in effect, like the sanitary inspectors the British colonial administrators employed elsewhere in the British Empire: they typically descended unannounced on African households and ordered the occupants to clean up their premises, their persons, and so forth, and generally bossed them around in the most high-handed fashion. Although they also gave lessons on cooking, dressmaking, and other useful matters, they were much resented, even hated, by their victims, who were not convinced that their newly acquired skills—like how to make nice scones—were worth the price they had to pay in the loss of dignity and mastery of their persons and homes.

Another mission strategy for preparing African women as exemplars of civilized behavior had a lasting social effect; it was the introduction of the social club, where the women met regularly for mutual reinforcement and dialogue, and to put their acquired Western manners to use. The earliest of these were the Ruwadzano clubs, which originated in the Wesleyan Methodist Church, and the largest of which, Rukwadzano rwe Wadzimayi (Women's Fellowship), was formed in 1929 at the Old Umtali Mission, and affiliated with the United Methodist Church (see chapter 7).[31]

WOMEN IN LIBERATION

Although the most active and most visible participants in the nationalist movement were men, women also played a significant role. One of their earliest significant actions was the huge 1962 demonstration against discrimination and political detentions. Two thousand demonstrators were arrested, and after their refusal to pay the fines assessed against them, they were imprisoned with their children. Undaunted, they continued their protest in prison, singing, destroying prison property, and generally disrupting the prison operations, until they were eventually released. As films like *Flame* (1996) show, numerous women also participated actively in the armed struggle for Zimbabwe's independence, including as combatants. Although initially excluded from the ranks of combat fighters, they were eventually admitted, and in time accounted for 25 to 30 percent of the fighters. By the end of the conflict some 10,000 women were under arms. Notable among them was Teurai Ropa Nhongo, who joined the Zimbabwe African National Liberation Army (ZANLA) at the age of seventeen and later assumed command of the Women's Detachment, a command she maintained even during a pregnancy. She later became the minister of youth, sports, and recreation in the independent Zimbabwe government, and eventually minister of community development and women's affairs. Other less celebrated women served as spies, hid munitions, cooked and sewed for the fighters, and raised funds for the struggle.

POST-INDEPENDENCE RELIEF

After independence, the Mugabe government moved quickly to remove the worst of the impediments the colonial government had imposed on Zimbabwe's women, one of its first actions being to pass a law granting unpaid maternity leave. The government established the Ministry of Community Development and Women's Affairs in 1981, and in cooperation with UNICEF it embarked on a program of building day-care facilities. In the following year the Legal Age of Majority Act emancipated women from the perpetual status of minors and freed them from the necessity to seek the permission of legal guardians to marry. They also ceased to be wards of their husbands. The Matrimonial Causes Act (1985) gave married women an interest in family property in cases of divorce, and the Civil Marriage Act (1985) brought all marriage, civil or traditional, within its purview. It allows for polygamy in unregistered traditional marriages, and with some restrictions in registered traditional ones. It does not, however, permit polygamy in civil marriages. Also in 1982, the government passed a law to guarantee equal pay for men and women for the same or comparable work. The main complaint the director of *Flame* dramatizes in her movie, though, is that, just as female combatants were subjected to some abuse by their male comrades, so after independence their rewards have not nearly equaled those the men, at least the highly placed men, have enjoyed.

WOMEN'S ORGANIZATIONS

The Ministry of National Affairs, Employment Creation and Co-operatives maintains a Department of Women's Affairs, but independently, women have organized several professional and community-based organizations to promote their interests and welfare. The list is long, but the following are a few of them: Women's Action Group; the Association of Women's Clubs of Zimbabwe; Zimbabwe Women's Resource Centre and Network; the National Federation of Business and Professional Women of Zimbabwe; Women in Business and Skills Development in Zimbabwe; Women in Law and Development in Africa; Zimbabwe Women Lawyers Association; Women Filmmakers of Zimbabwe; the Zimbabwe Association of University Women; Gays and Lesbians of Zimbabwe; Women and AIDS Support Network; and many more.

In April 1999, a Supreme Court ruling on the status of women caused consternation in Zimbabwe's women and feminist circles, because it supposedly removed the constitutional provision granting women equal status with men, and decreed instead that a woman had only the status of a "junior male." An alert issued by the Sisterhood Is Global Institute (SIGI) on its Web site on June 30, 1999, gave the details of the case that led to the ruling. A fifty-eight-year-old Shona woman had sued her half-brother for the inheritance of their deceased father's land, and the Supreme Court had ruled, according to the site, that "women should not be able to inherit land 'because of the consideration in the African society which, among other factors, was to the effect that women were not able to look after their original family (of birth) because of their commitment to the new family (through marriage).' " It seemed as though Zimbabwe was going against the trend of removing obstacles in the path of women's aspirations, but the same SIGI alert published a letter (dated May 26, 1999) from a registrar of the Supreme Court explaining that the ruling simply affirmed the pertinent Shona Customary Law that was in force. It apparently did not affect the gains women have achieved under the country's constitution and legal statutes.

THE IMPACT OF AIDS

While traditional societies in the country frowned on promiscuity on the part of both men and women, the modern lifestyle is more tolerant of the indulgence, on the part of men especially, but also on that of women. One of the latest problems women have had to contend with, partly as a consequence of the new permissiveness and promiscuity, is the AIDS epidemic. Zimbabwe is one of the countries hardest hit in Africa, and the high incidence of the disease, especially among men, is making widows of many young married women, who must unexpectedly assume the roles of household manager, caregiver, and breadwinner. They also face the unenviable and difficult task of putting pressure on their men to abandon high-risk activities like extramarital affairs.

NOTES

1. Olivia N. Muchena, "Zimbabwe: It Can Only Be Handled by Women," in *Sisterhood Is Global: The International Women's Movement Anthology*, ed. Robin Morgan (New York: Anchor, 1984), 752.
2. Supriya Nair, "Melancholic Women: The Intellectual Hysteric(s) in *Nervous Conditions*," *Research in African Literatures* 26, no. 2 (Summer 1995): 136–37.
3. Patricia Cheney, *The Land and People of Zimbabwe* (New York: J. B. Lippincott, 1990), 203.
4. Charles Bullock, *The Mashona (The Indigenous Natives of S. Rhodesia)* (1928; reprint, Westport, CT: Negro Universities Press, 1970), 248.
5. Sekai Nzenza-Shand, *Songs to an African Sunset: A Zimbabwean Story* (Melbourne: Lonely Planet Publications, 1997), 215.
6. Bullock, 248–49.
7. Ibid., 249–50.
8. Buchi Emecheta, *The Slave Girl* (New York: George Braziller, 1977), 177–79.
9. Cheney, 197.
10. Bullock, 220.
11. Ibid.
12. Ibid., 217n.
13. Chenjerai Hove, *Bones* (Oxford: Heinemann, 1991), 93.
14. Ibid., 98.
15. Ibid., 97.
16. Nzenza-Shand, 70.

17. Ibid., 215.

18. Mariama Bâ, *So Long a Letter* (London: Heinemann, 1981), 58.

19. Nzenza-Shand, 235.

20. Ibid., 85.

21. Robin Morgan, ed., *Sisterhood Is Global: The International Women's Movement Anthology* (New York: Anchor, 1984), 750.

22. Michael Gelfand, *Shona Religion, with Special Reference to the Makorekore* (Cape Town, Wynberg, and Johannesburg: Juta and Co., 1962), 55.

23. Nzenza-Shand, 59.

24. Ibid., 117–18.

25. Ibid., 143.

26. Ibid., 142–45.

27. Muchena, 753.

28. Timothy Burke, *Lifebuoy Men, Lux Women: Commodification, Consumption, and Cleanliness in Modern Zimbabwe* (Durham: Duke University Press, 1996), 44–45.

29. Teresa Barnes, " 'Am I a Man?': Gender and the Pass Laws in Urban Colonial Zimbabwe, 1930–80," *African Studies Review* 40, no. 1 (April 1997): 73.

30. Ibid.

31. R. Kent Rasmussen and Steven C. Rubert, *Historical Dictionary of Zimbabwe*, 2 ed. (Metuchen, NJ: Scarecrow, 1990).

7

Social Customs and Lifestyle

THE INDIVIDUAL IN THE COMMUNITY

THE EMPHASIS ON THE COMMUNITY in African traditional social organization does not diminish the importance and value of the individual and his or her role therein; indeed, in the end traditional African life was organized to ensure the security, safety, and well-being of every human being. Whatever ritual or ceremony we might examine, we will find that its end in some way serves one of two broad functions: to formally establish the place and role of the individual or individuals concerned in the scheme of things, in order to maintain harmony and good order among humans; and to ensure the good disposition of the supernatural powers toward the community and its constituent individuals, in order that they might continue to offer their protection and blessing. The elaborate celebrations that attend the rites of passage are a testimony to the importance society attaches to them. In the following pages we will take a look at such ceremonies, from the time an individual makes an entry into the world until he or she takes leave of it, demonstrating in the process that in Zimbabwe, as elsewhere in Africa, life begins before birth, and continues after death.

CHILDBIRTH

Preparation for Birth

Motherhood confers considerable importance on women that no other status (wifehood, or the like) approximates. Therefore, when a woman becomes pregnant she and the child she is carrying receive considerable

pampering. The baby becomes the subject of communal attention and concern well before its birth, but the real fuss focuses on the expectant mother
(Chishona—the language of the shona—*chirema*). She goes on a diet that
excludes things bitter or sour, and she must also closely watch where she
goes, what she does, and what she sees. She must not look at anything bad,
physical deformities for example, lest her child be similarly deformed, and
neither she nor her husband may kill a snake, lest the child be born blind.
She must also stay away from cattle kraals and other people's farms, because
Shona people believe that her condition might cause some sort of misfortune to befall herds or crops she might come in contact with.[1] She spends
the last month of her pregnancy alone with the midwife in a specially prepared hut, preferably in her mother's village, and she must avoid all contact
with her husband. For his part, the husband deposits some of his clothes in
the hut, which, however, must be thrown out at the onset of labor.

Labor and Delivery

The normal expectation is that labor and delivery will be uneventful, as long,
that is, as the powers that control the universe, in particular the ancestors, are
in good humor. Any untoward occurrence therefore indicates a supernatural
intervention. One common assumption is that an ancestor is displeased because the woman had been involved in illicit sexual activity, and she must di-
vulge the identity of her paramour before she can be safely delivered. In the
past a mild form of torture was applied to encourage confession: a split bamboo roofing bough was tightly bound round her head, and its end was tapped
until she confessed.[2] Refusal to confess could prove fatal. The practice according to which an expectant mother returns to her mother's village for delivery offers her a measure of protection in such circumstances, for her own
kin would conceal whatever indiscretion she might confess from her husband
and his family, thus avoiding any awkwardness or danger to the woman.

Prolonged or complicated labor does not always mean that the woman
has committed an offense, though, as the difficulty might be an indication
that an ancestor wishes to convey a message to the living. The fictionalized
account of Mapondera's birth in Mutswairo's novel is a case in point. Worried by her patient's long and painful labor, the likes of which she had never
seen in all her years of practice, the midwife told Mapondera's father that a
ngozi spirit was blocking his wife's delivery. From her training and long experience she recognized the signs that an ancestor was somehow aggrieved,
and she urged that a medium be sought to intercede with the ancestors and
ascertain the cause of the grievance. Having offered the necessary sacrifice to
the spirits, the medium received a visit from the ghost of Chaminuka, who

stated that the child to be born was destined to be the hero who would deliver his people from their enemies.[3]

When birth is imminent, another midwife is called in to help with the delivery. Afterward, the chief midwife receives the child and offers an ululation, and the people waiting outside the hut respond in kind, thus broadcasting the news of the happy event. The new mother enters into a new social status: she is now no longer *chirema* but "she who has given birth." The family sacrifices a goat to the ancestors, and the women of the household eat it, sharing it with the new mother and the midwives, who get the choicest parts.

Postpartum Care

The midwives partially cut the new baby's umbilical cord but leave a bit attached to the navel. In many African societies the cord has considerable psychic significance. Many believe that no matter how long people live and no matter how far they travel away from home, the placenta will always pull them back to the place where it was buried. Accordingly, the Ndebele bury the cord and the placenta right under the floor of the hut where the child was born. The Shona do not seem to attach the same value to the umbilical cord, although it does have some significance. For example, the father is barred from seeing the child until the cord has healed. In some Shona groups, unmarried girls may see a newborn only after it has been washed and the placenta carefully disposed of by the older women attending the birth. After the remnant of the cord has fallen off, the baby is carefully bathed, rubbed down with oil, shaved, and named.

When her work is done, the midwife takes her leave, taking with her all the materials she has worked with, including all the clothes the new mother wore during labor and the ones the father left in the hut. If he makes the mistake of entering the hut before the time when he is authorized to do so, the midwife may seize the clothes he is wearing also. This is supposedly done for the mother's good, but in fact constitutes a supplement to the midwife's fees, which she assesses according to the man's means.

NAMING

Different Shona groups observe different schedules and procedures for naming new babies. In some groups no ceremony is involved; the father simply names the child a few days after its birth. In others the timing is specified (for example, after the umbilical cord has become detached), but no special ceremony attends the event. In yet others a ceremony is mandatory. Sometimes the midwife names the child, squirting it with water from her mouth and pronouncing the name the mother has provided. In the case of Mapondera, the child was named immediately after birth, with no attendant ceremony, the given name expressing the family's (and the people's) expectation of him. But in this case the father, not the mother, supplied the name, which accorded with Chaminuka's earlier revelation about the child, that "he shall be the *mupundi*—the destroyer—the great warrior."[4]

CHILDHOOD

The baby is not technically a human being with a soul until he or she cuts the first teeth. When that happens, both the baby and the mother enter into a new status: the mother becomes *mai* (mother), and the child *mucheche* (a little person).[5] With achieved humanity come duties and the commencement of the socialization process that will make him or her a responsible and worthy member of the society.

Education and Early Socialization

Socialization involves learning the rules and principles of proper behavior and understanding one's duties and obligations, largely through attentive observation of the actions and behavior of role models. Traditional education in Africa is informal, practical, and closely integrated with daily living, and begins from the time children are able to understand the world around them. Girls and boys learn from the achievement of cognition that they are destined for different roles and responsibilities in society. They observe older relatives of the same gender and emulate their habits. In some cases there may be structured instruction from father to son, or, in Shona society, from grandfather to grandson, especially with regard to specific skills, but that is not to be construed as anything like regular schooling sessions for a period set aside each day for that purpose, and for a set number of years, after which the child "graduated." Boys accompany and observe their fathers or grandfathers in their different pursuits, and receive explanations and instructions from older siblings. In time they begin to attempt the activities themselves, initially under observation, until they become proficient and can strike out on their own. The same goes for girls, who come under the tutelage of their mothers, grandmothers, and aunts.

In Zimbabwe, education is much more than the acquisition of skills; it involves such things as self-care, comportment, and the like. Children learn personal cleanliness early, and "by the age of four the child should have learnt the use of the right hand, the use of good language, clapping hands and cleanliness."[6] They learn very early, for example, that it is very bad form to eat before washing their hands; they learn that they may not bathe where adults are bathing, for they must not see older people naked;[7] they learn the demands of etiquette, for example that younger people must go to their elders in the morning to greet them, and that "a boy, on coming to grown men sitting at the *dare*, should sit down, clap his hands and say, 'We greet you, old ones.' "[8] And as soon as they are capable of learning anything, they learn that when they come upon people, even strangers, on the path, good breeding requires that they exchange greetings with them.

By the age of six a young boy's older brothers give him a wooden axe and toy bow. He now eats with them and shares the unmarried men's sleeping hut with them, and he begins to help them herding livestock. The older boys teach him about plants and animals and how to snare birds with birdlime, and eventually he gets a real bow. He also joins the older ones in their other chores on the farm and around the kraal: cultivating corn, building and thatching huts, building the firewood storage stalls, making wooden spoons and porridge stirrers, and hunting rats.[9]

These, then, are the days when the foundations are laid for later professions, and, therefore, for paying particular attention to the acquisition of the necessary skills, whether as ironsmith, professional hunter, or accomplished farmer, professions to which the society attaches as much importance as to those of the king, the medicine man, and the medium, either in terms of the effort they require or of the rituals they involve.

As for young girls, they accompany their mothers and grandmothers to pick herbs, vegetables, and mushrooms, and learn how to gather edible termites and how to cook *sadza* (porridge). By the time they are ten they have learned all they need to know about wifely duties, and it is not uncommon, in traditional Shona society, for a girl to move into her husband's village by the age of ten. Their other duties include making pots for carrying water, for cooking, and for the relish that accompanies *sadza*. They are also responsible for polishing the floors of the huts, making the platform for storing pots and baskets, and taking care of the goats' pen.[10]

The society recognizes excellence by giving special titles to those who have demonstrated exceptional skill in their professions: "*Mhidzá* is the title given to any craftsman skilled in the arts of weaving, carving, and the building of houses, granaries, and other structures. The special titles of *maridzangoma* and *maridzambira* apply to the drummer and the mbira player, whose services are in demand at dances of all kinds, especially those held to invoke and invite the visitation of the spirits."[11] Similarly, women skilled in pottery and brewing are honored with the title *mhizhá* or *nyanzví*.

African societies place a premium on the mastery of speech and the nuances of proper communication and the artistic use of language. The Shona are not an exception, for they encourage their youth to engage in creative composition and to become *nyandúri*, the designation society confers on those who show a discriminating knowledge of language and its proper use and those with poetic talent.[12] The youth cultivate their skill through storytelling sessions, and under the tutelage of their parents and grandparents. Such is the weight attached to this activity that children may not be sent on errands that might interfere with storytelling, posing and solving riddles, or participating in song and play. Other training opportunities arise when boys play house with girls and frolic with them at bathing places, on which occasions they practice composing love poems. Furthermore, when they engage in mock combats among themselves, they exercise their wit at fighting boasts and clan praises.

Initiation and the End of Traditional Cadethood

To reiterate, although there is nothing in traditional education that, like formal Western schooling, is calibrated into progressive steps and assigned a certain number of years, generally, traditional youths in fact also receive their education and socialization in their early years, in late childhood and young adulthood. And just as Western education is formally rounded off with graduation, so in many cultures its traditional counterpart also concludes ceremonially with initiation. The ceremony formally marks transition from childhood and its attendant limitations on social responsibilities, obligations, and possibilities, to adulthood and the right to unrestricted participation in the affairs of the community.

Not all cultures have initiation ceremonies, though, and in those that do they vary widely. In general, male cadets go through the ritual in age groups, the same groups in which they would, if called upon, go into battle as a regiment, participate in communal projects, and so forth. They maintain their group ties for life and develop a bond of fellowship with its members that is sometimes as strong as the one they have for their blood kin, if not stronger.

Initiation generally involves some instruction, which the male novices receive at the *dare*. It usually includes demonstration of manly mettle, and circumcision. The instructors are the boys' maternal uncles and their wives. What the novices get is in essence a crash recapitulation of what they have thus far internalized by experience with regard to social mores: the importance of cleanliness and the like, proper deference, regard and respect for elders, respect for other people's property and for other men's wives or betrothed, and how to be good husbands. The boys may be instructed as follows:

"Obey the old!"
"In all circumstances and at all times, respect the old. If you meet them, leave the path and so show respect. If you go towards the *korono*

[where men sit] where they sit, kneel down (but as a man kneels) and *losha* [offer salutation]. Put your hands together in front of your breast, and bow your head. . . . Not until you have received the permission *Dzulani zwanu chibanda* may you sit down."[13]

In some cultures the ceremony takes place in seclusion; among the Venda the site is a camp hidden in the bush, and what happens there is kept secret. The event occupies three months, during which the novice sleeps in the open without a blanket and eats a Spartan diet. Its culmination is the circumcision, and after the operation the initiates receive the medicine for their treatment from their uncles.

Among the Ndebele, after a boy has his first wet dream, he rises before all others early the next morning and goes naked to bathe in the stream. On his return he stands outside the homestead near the approach to the cattle kraals. On seeing him there, his comrades beat him with sticks and chase him into the bush, and there he remains for two or three days, eating only at night, before returning home. A ceremony follows in which he eats special food, and a medicine man gives him maize meal at the end of a stick, which he must take with his mouth. After that the medicine man gives him three or four blows of the stick to harden him. The ceremony ends with the boy's father and relatives giving him presents of cattle, sheep, and goats.

The women charged with safeguarding the clan's charms and preparing women for marriage are responsible for seeing young women through the rite of initiation. They impart moral and physical instruction to candidates regarding wifehood, and enjoin chastity, which they also monitor by surveillance and occasional inspection. They also teach their wards culinary arts. At the end of the instruction period, they brew beer and give a feast for the parents. A woman is ready for marriage after her first menstruation. When the event occurs, the woman washes herself profusely in cold water, and a few days later her parents give a feast in her honor. Thereafter she can wear the full skirt that indicates her readiness for marriage.

MARRIAGE

The Importance of Children

To anyone familiar with African cultures it would come as no surprise that among the Shona the main purpose of marriage is to procreate and continue the blood line. With them "the object of marriage, and of their lives firstly, secondly and thirdly" is bearing children.[14] If a wife fails in this regard, the husband may ask her father to return the cattle he gave as the *lobola*, or for another wife. Because of the paramount importance of procreation, the culture permits a man to sleep with his prospective wife before they are considered married, and if no pregnancy results he is fully entitled to return her to her family and recover his *lobola* or be given another daughter in replacement. If it can be established that the failure is on the man's part, the families concerned make discreet arrangements for a relative of his to impregnate the woman, and the resulting children will be her husband's.

Courtship

As with other rituals, there is no uniformity in courtship rituals among the different Zimbabwe groups, or even among the various Shona subgroups. In some cases, a young man desiring a wife approaches his uncle, who approaches his father on his behalf. His mother then brews some beer and gives a feast, after which the search for a suitable woman takes place. When she has been identified, all that remains is the agreement of terms between the two families, and no further ceremony is required. In other cases, though, certain formal steps ensue.

Among the Korekore, the male suitor takes the initiative, his first approach being to the woman of his choice. He approaches her when she is at work with her parents and makes a show of helping. The parents take their cue and withdraw, and the two young people talk. He offers her a token, and, if she is agreeable, she accepts it and informs her mother, who in turn informs her father. If the young woman spurns the young man's advances he must leave her alone. Her positive response obliges the father to follow suit, as long as he is satisfied that the suitor comes from a good home; otherwise the young woman must return the token. Only after the suitor has been accepted does he inform his parents, and his father must likewise be satisfied with the prospective wife's parentage before any union can take place.

Among the Zezuru it is an elderly male relative of the prospective groom who informs the chosen woman's father of the young man's interest; the latter accepts a token of agreement, which may be a bracelet or a hoe, and consults his relatives. Once the woman's father accepts the token, the woman is considered the young man's wife.

The Intermediary

In those cases where further ceremony is mandated, after the initial contact has taken place and the young man has received the signal to press his suit, custom requires that he appoint an intermediary (*dombo*) to act on his behalf. Among the Korekore the process continues as follows: the woman's father convenes a family council in which the intermediary presents the token to him in the presence of his brothers and other close relatives; the woman herself may be present or absent, but if present she does not speak. The father shows the token to the young woman's mother, and then summons his daughter to indicate her consent to the union by accepting the token. That done, the father tells the emissary to invite the suitor to the village. Acceptance of the token in fact seals the marriage, although the couple does not live together until other ceremonies have taken place.

The suitor goes to the woman's village with his brothers, each bearing a bundle of firewood as gift, and he remains behind when his brothers return home. For the next three weeks he serves his parents-in-law, doing such chores as sweeping the *dare* and lighting the fire in the morning. He is not yet permitted to live with his bride, but must share sleeping quarters with his brothers-in-law. At the end of the period and at the request of his father-in-law, he summons his family and relatives to perform *binza*, that is, tasks such as weeding the garden, uprooting trees, thatching huts, and so forth. The tasks occupy them from about 6 A.M. until about 3 P.M. Afterwards their host kills a goat, a pig, and a fowl for a feast, which the bride and her mother take to the workers in the field. Their host comes to thank them, and they return to their village, leaving the groom with his wife. Only now do the couple get their own hut in which they can live as man and wife. The young man remains in the village until his wife becomes pregnant, at which point he takes her home to his village.

The arrangement by which the couple live with the bride's family is the oldest form of marriage among the Shona. A different form prevails among the Zezuru. After the suitor has settled on his choice for a spouse, he sends his emissary to take cattle and three hoes to the woman's father; he himself visits her village to help her mother with chores and to give her gifts. Here too, he sweeps the *dare* and lights the morning fire. When the time is appropriate, he sends another hoe to his prospective father-in-law to ask for his bride. At this point her mother gives her some meal and a small jar of oil, and sends her off with an uncle, an older female relative, and at least one younger sister (carrying a pot of water) to her new home. The uncle leads the way to the village and announces her arrival while she is still at the outskirts. When the women of the village come out to receive her, she kneels down and covers her face; they give her small presents and urge her to reveal her beauty, which she does with a show of reluctance. The women ululate and call out her family name in appreciation. The bride sleeps with the bridal party that night, and the following morning the young woman who carried the pot of water presents it to the husband's relatives to wash their hands. The marriage is now finalized, and the party departs, leaving the bride in her new home.[15]

Marriage by Elopement

Another form of Shona marriage is known as *ku tiza makumbo*; it is marriage by elopement. The term means "to flee (by) legs," and it has a variant, *ku tizisa makumbo*, which means "to cause the legs to flee."[16] The young man approaches the woman at a song and dance party (*chi-imbo*) and they agree on their escapade. They arrange to meet the next day, and when they do the woman gives the man a love token and they set the date for their elopement. On the appointed day, he takes her to his village, and she sits on the outskirts, covering her head with a blanket. The womenfolk signal that she is welcome by giving her bracelets and lifting the blanket. She may then enter the village as a guest, but not the groom's hut, for she is not yet his bride.

The man now sends his intermediary to the woman's parents with the gift of a hoe. He takes care not to enter the village, but calls from afar to let the people know what has become of their daughter. He then flees, leaving the hoe behind. The woman's parents send some stalwarts after their daughter, and they take her back home after breaking a few things at the man's village. After a few days, she runs away to the man's village again. This time the groom's messenger boldly presents the hoe to her father, and if he agrees to the marriage, he accepts it and arranges to visit his new son-in-law's village, where they come to an agreement on the number of *lobola* cattle he will receive. The young man may now build his own hut and take in his bride.

As the foregoing description indicates, the process involves a good deal of sport. It is in fact something of a drama that the two groups (the groom's and the bride's families) engage in once the initial actions of the couple have alerted them to what is afoot. Thereafter, each participant takes his/her cue and acts according to a set script. In this sense, what is described as "elopement" represents something quite different from what the word signifies in a Western context. *Ku tiza makumbo* is, in effect, another more or less formal marriage ritual.

The Importance of Chastity

The society's emphasis on chastity on the part of the woman is apparent in the provision that permits the groom to seek assurance that his wife is a virgin at the time of their marriage. In the case of the Korekore, the groom does so after the *binza* and before his family departs for their own village. The task of ascertaining the bride's condition is assigned to two women, one from each family. If their finding is favorable, the groom arranges to perform the *masungiro* ceremony, in essence a ceremony of gratitude, a week later. For this he procures two goats and an ox from his village and prepares a feast. One of the goats is for the medicine expended on the woman as she grew up, and the other is to compensate her mother for all her trouble in raising her. Some southern Shona groups perform the *masungiro* if the wife is already pregnant, or if the marriage has already been consummated.[17]

With regard to the Zezuru, the older women of the village take charge of the woman after she has lifted her blanket, and lead her to the stream for examination. If they find her to be unchaste, they present a pierced hoe, a sign of disgrace, to the bridal party, who take the unfortunate woman back home. Her family must then find who her lover was and make him pay a fine, say, a cow, which accompanies her back to her prospective husband. Sometimes a younger sister (as a bride to the husband) is the price her father must pay. If the bride is found to be chaste, the groom kills a goat and sends some of the meat to his mother-in-law.

The observation (and objection) that in neither case is the man's chastity an issue is legitimate, and one can speculate that the explanation resides in the fact that indiscretion on the part of the woman might result in her bearing a child that does not "belong" by blood to her husband. A case can be made, nevertheless, for gender inequity.

DEATH AND FUNERARY RITES

The traditional African society consists of the living, those yet to be born, and those who have lived and died. The dead, especially those who lived to a mature age and who had children before dying, are especially important because they constitute the community of ancestors, and they exert considerable influence over the affairs of the living. They maintain a close watch on their living relatives, who in turn must humor them with occasional offerings of sacrifices and by avoiding actions that are offensive to the departed. For the traditional African, therefore, the prospect of dying is not as frightening as it might be if he or she believed that death puts a final end to existence; it is in fact a welcome transition to another form of "living," free of the cares and limitations of this life.

In connection with childbirth we saw how the family of the baby about to be born takes steps to ease its entry into the world, and we have seen how the rites of initiation and the ceremonies pertaining to marriage ensure an orderly life for the adult person. The people similarly handle a person's dying with solemnity and care, because they wish to ensure his or her spirit a safe passage and happy integration into the community of the ancestors. Funerary rituals are important not only for the dying but also for the survivors, for just as the post-mortality well-being of the dying person is at stake, so are the survivors' prospects of receiving favorable attention, rather than neglect or even possible angry visitations, from the deceased ancestor. As a way of cementing the link between the living and the spirit of the dead, a nephew of the dying person (and to a lesser extent a niece) takes a prominent role in the funerary rituals.

The rites typically break down into four ceremonies spanning a period of two years. They begin with the actual burial and end with the distribution of the deceased person's property after he or she has achieved ancestor status. The first ceremony (at the actual burial) is called *kuviga*; the second, which takes place about a month after death, is *mharadzo*; the third, *kurova guva* or *kutamba guva*, occurs about a year or two after death; and the last, *nhaka* (inheritance), takes place a day after the *kurova guva*.

Kuviga

When a man dies, his wife or wives wash his body with the help of a nephew, lay it on a mat in the hut, and cover it with a fiber blanket. It is not unusual nowadays to use an ordinary blanket. The body lies in the hut for no more than twenty-four hours, during which time relatives visit the deceased, drop monetary or jewelry gifts into a plate next to the body, and ask for his protection. In the meantime, the nephew, along with the ritual friend of the deceased, will have gone in the late afternoon to select a burial spot. At the end of the lying-in-state, the ritual friend, with the help of three other men, carries the body on a stretcher to the grave in the company of a procession of singing, chanting, and jumping mourners. Along the way the carriers place the body on the ground three times, each time with the head pointing in the direction of the village. Thereafter, they point the head in the direction of the grave.

The grave is usually cut in an anthill about a mile from the village, and is about eight feet deep and three or four feet square at the opening. The ritual friend's last duty is to position the body in the grave, after which he departs, and the men left behind fill the entrance with stones, and the rest with soil. Next, the nephew and a niece approach the grave, beside which is a large pot which the dead man used in life for his bath water, a calabash from which he drank, the wooden plate from which he ate, and his pillow. The nephew mixes some millet meal and water in the calabash and pours it on the grave just above the head of the deceased, and prays to Chikara to receive the spirit of the man he has called away. On his instruction the women sit down and ululate while the men clap their hands. All then return to the village for the funeral feast, for which a bull is killed.

The people believe that some time after a dead person is buried, his or her spirit emerges from the grave and wanders about until it is time for it to be called to rejoin the family as an ancestor. When a corpse is buried, therefore, a long stick is rested against the body such that after the grave has been filled the top of the stick will be visible above ground. It will be pulled out after the earth has settled in the grave, usually after several months, leaving a hole through which the spirit of the dead can emerge, which it does as a caterpillar or a worm. After the removal of the stick a relative visits the grave periodically to watch for the emergence of the spirit. The belief is that once it emerges, the spirit wanders about, and preparations can begin to welcome it home at the *kurova guva* (or *bira*) ceremony.

Within forty-eight hours of the burial, the ritual friend and a blood relative of the deceased go to the grave to see if it has been disturbed. If they discover anything amiss, such as a hole, the ritual friend informs the head of the family, who arranges for rectification. If the grave has been desecrated the suspicion is that a witch is responsible, and the family consults a *n'anga*. Even if the grave has not been disturbed, the people's concern that the person's death involved no foul play is so strong that the consultation of a *n'anga* for assurance is a constant, and is in fact the main feature of the second funerary ceremony, the *mharadzo*.

Mharadzo

For the *mharadzo* (or *kudzira*), which occurs a month or two after the burial, women brew beer in a special way, and the survivors take some to the grave, where they offer some of it to the deceased and drink the rest. On the following day, the deceased's eldest son asks his uncle, usually the oldest man in the family, to consult a *n'anga* to ascertain that his father's death was from natural causes. The uncle usually choses a *n'anga* in a distant village, in order to ensure that he would have no knowledge of the family or its affairs. In the past, if the *n'anga* discovered that a witch was responsible for the death he named the miscreant and prepared medicine for the survivors' protection. They (and the community) made the accused witch undergo an ordeal to prove his innocence. If he failed he was axed to death and his body thrown into the river. His family then had to flee the village. If he passed, his relatives demanded compensation, usually a daughter from the accusing family. Nowadays the law prohibits the *n'anga*, for obvious reasons, from revealing the identity of the witch.

Kurova guva (Kutamba Guva)

The *kurova guva* or *kutamba guva*, which takes place a year or two after the deceased's death, is essentially the same as the *mharadzo*. This is the ceremony in which the wandering spirit of the dead is invited back to rejoin the family as an ancestor, and a celebration of the return of the spirit to the homestead. It also presages the final settlement of the deceased's affairs as a person, during the final ceremony of *nhaka*. The *kurova guva* is therefore a festive, forward-looking ceremony, for afterwards the survivors are released from mourning, they share the deceased person's property among them, and the widow(s) may remarry or resume life unattached.

By the time the *kurova guva* takes place the family will have selected a relative of the deceased as his spirit medium. In some cases the choice automatically falls on the oldest son, but the spirit may choose its own medium (indicating his choice through an illness and a diagnosis by a *n'anga*). Ten days before the occasion, village elders and close relatives of the dead person gather at the granary and inform the ancestors that they are preparing for the event. Then the sisters of the dead person set about the all-important task of brewing the special beer for the ceremony. A night of singing and dancing precedes the procession to the grave site on the appointed day.

The following morning, the celebrants pour a libation on the grave and inform the dead person that his survivors are preparing to welcome his spirit home, and that on that day one of his children will be appointed to carry his name. Alternatively, he may be asked to choose his own medium (if none has been chosen). They also remind him that as the living are fulfilling their role, he should also fulfil his as their spiritual protector.

Meanwhile, back at the homestead the husband of the dead man's oldest sister slaughters an ox. The meat is roasted and the mourners eat it, along with the boiled blood. Then everyone gathers around the well-guarded clay pots containing the special beer. They inspect them for any cracks, which would suggest that the spirit of the dead person is displeased and must be appeased. After determining that the spirit is happy, the people drink the beer in celebration. Another method of determining whether the spirit is pleased or displeased is for the relatives to take several pots of beer to the cattle kraal and pour some over a bull's head. If the animal shakes off the beer, the spirit is happy, but if it does not, they pour another pot on it until it does shake its head. When that happens, the people gathered celebrate, the women ululating to signal the grand finale of the ceremony.

Nhaka

The ceremony of *nhaka*, which takes place the day after the *kurova guva* and can be seen as an extension of it, is a family affair for the express purpose of distributing the deceased's property among his descendants. It is another festive occasion, anticipating the final end of mourning and the resumption of normal life for all concerned. The important business of the occasion begins with the invitation to the widow to jump over some of her dead husband's possessions. If she trips she is exposed as having engaged in sexual affairs since her husband's death, but if she jumps cleanly, she is "clean" and ready again for matrimony. That business taken care of, the disposition (or release) of the wife follows. Tradition provides for younger male relatives of her dead husband to vie for her, provided that she is agreeable to the arrangement. Each suitor presents a bowl of water to her, and if she accepts him, she takes it and uses the water (for example, presenting it to the suitor to wash his hands); if she does not, she throws out the water. She does not have to accept someone from the dead husband's family, and may choose to live as a free woman or marry whomever else she chooses. In some cases, a woman elects to be "inherited" by her own son, an arrangement that formally places her under his protection and shields her from unwanted male attention.

Ndebele Funerary Practice

Ndebele rites are remarkably similar to Shona ones. When an Ndebele person falls ill, relatives, including the eldest son and at least one brother, keep a vigil at the bedside. They are responsible for investigating the cause of the illness (magic or witchcraft) and for seeking a cure. The oldest son's presence symbolizes the continuation of the person's life in his children, who will keep him in remembrance. If the person's condition shows no improvement after those caring for him have done all they can, the relatives may kill "the beast of the ancestors," an ox or a goat kept for the purpose, in order to hasten death and terminate pain. The slaughter also connects the sick person to the departed, and symbolizes the impending festive union of the dying person with those who went before.

After the person's death, his brother begins to dig a grave oriented in an east-west position on uncultivated ground, and is later joined by others. They wrap the body in animal skin (a blanket is now an acceptable option), and if the deceased is the head of a household they carry the body out through a hole in the wall and an opening in the fence surrounding the homestead, as it must not be taken through the door or through the fence gate. The purpose is to preserve the notion that the head of the household has not in fact departed it.[18] Men lead the funeral procession carrying the corpse, and the women follow. People avoid meeting such a procession, because it is considered an ill omen. At the grave site the oldest son strikes the grave with a spear (symbolically fighting off any enemies the dead might encounter on his way), and the bearers of the body lay it in the grave, the head facing south. If the deceased is a woman, they lay the body on her left side;

if a man, they lay him on his right side. They place some personal belongings in the grave before they fill it with earth, and place thorny branches on top to keep animals and witches away.

Back home, the family kills either an ox (for a man) or a goat (for a woman) to accompany the deceased. They roast the meat and eat it without salt, then they completely burn the bones to ashes and mix them into a medicine for the survivors to drink. Each person swallows one mouthful and spits out the second. They then go to the river to wash, and after that they disperse, with the exception of the oldest son and the brother, who spend the night at the homestead, and two or three women relatives or friends, who will participate in the formal wailing on the day following the funeral.

The following morning, the deceased's brother and the oldest son go to inspect the grave. If they find it undisturbed they assume that the death was from natural causes; otherwise they summon a diviner to find out the cause of death and what measures must be taken.

The ceremony of "washing the hoes," which is the equivalent of the Shona *mharadzo*, takes place one to three months after the burial. The ceremony's name derives from the fact that the mourners wash the implements they used for the burial with beer, in addition to administering medicine to the children of the household. The ceremony (*umbiyiso*) to welcome the spirit back into the family as an ancestor follows a year later for men and women who were married before dying. It compares to the Shona *kurova guva*. The survivors kill an ox, cook its meat, and reserve it for the next day. All night they drink special beer brewed from maize grown after the deceased's death and seeds obtained from outside the homestead, eat, snuff tobacco communally, and address requests to the ancestor. They place the rest of the food and drink in front of the hut for the ancestor to consume, and in the morning they sing, "*Ubaba makeze ekhaya*" (Father come home!). They then eat the ox meat from the day before and drink more beer.

This festive occasion marks the end of all restrictions the death had imposed on the survivors and releases the widows to remarry. Relatives and friends feast and dance, and afterwards the relatives distribute the dead person's property among the survivors. Finally, they choose a new "beast of the ancestors," usually a black ox but never a sheep, and place it in the care of the main heir, usually the eldest son. The family must inform the animal of all important matters concerning its members, and periodically brew a small amount of beer and pour it on its head as an offering.

CHANGES IN ZIMBABWE CUSTOMS AND LIFESTYLES

The European presence in Zimbabwe has caused profound changes in the way the people live. The Europeans did not simply settle in the area to take advantage of the opportunities it offered for the good life; they intended, in addition, to transform it into a semblance of their ancestral home, and in the process convert Africans to European ways, at least to the extent that doing so served the Europeans' interests. For example, they reserved most of the arable land for themselves, and forced the African population into cramped and infertile enclaves. They otherwise induced them to seek employment on white-owned farms or in the urban centers, in both cases for meager wages. In any event, the new developments disrupted traditional African life by dispersing families, undermining long-established social mechanisms, and generally rendering the communities unstable.

The trend toward westernization began early, as the Africans who relocated to European-controlled areas assumed lifestyles appropriate to their new environment and status. They had quickly learned that the future belonged to those who embraced the new ways, and those who had an eye to the future found it expedient to accommodate themselves to the new circumstances. A few examples of the impact of the European presence follow, especially with regard to education and socialization. We will also see how, despite the urge to westernize, the pull of tradition continues to assert itself at crucial moments.

Colonial Education

When it assumed control of the Rhodesian territory in the 1890s, the British South Africa Company (BSAC) was more interested in the economic exploitation of the colony than in educating Africans, and the early white settlers shared the same priority. Accordingly, the 1899 ordinance creating a department of education provided for the education of whites only, not of Africans. It, however, offered inducements to Christian missions in the form of grants and land to establish segregated schools that would produce African workers to serve the white community in the agricultural and industrial sectors, and provide other services the settlers might require. In keeping with the Rhodesian authorities' general attitude toward Africans, throughout the colonial period the amount the government spent on educating an African child was a mere fraction of what it spent on other children, European, Asian, and colored, the inevitable result being the gross undereducation of the African population. Indeed, only a fraction of the African children of school age were enrolled in schools, and they were enrolled almost exclusively at the primary level. The picture worsened considerably when the freedom struggle began, because the government shut down the schools in combat zones for security reasons, and a large number of school children joined the freedom fighters.

The missionaries, to whom the early task of educating Africans fell, were not entirely satisfied with the arrangement; although they welcomed the subsidies from the government, they also believed in providing meaningful education to Africans. The Rhodesian Christian Conference continually pressured the colonial administration to pay greater attention to African education, but to little avail. Some African organizations took practical measures to alter the situation and, beginning in 1902, they started their own independent schools. An official reaction came in 1910, when the Graham Commission report (named for Sir James Graham) took note of the race-based discrepancy in youth education and recommended offering a limited range of diversified education to Africans. It proposed the inclusion of some academic subjects in the syllabus, while continuing, though, to stress practical education. The schools would continue to be administered by Christian missionaries, but with the stipulation that the education they provided must not encourage Africans to engage in actions that might create racial tensions. Two years later, the administration coupled this positive move with the negative step of outlawing the independent schools.

Beginning in the 1920s, the government began to operate its own primary schools, and in 1925 it established a Department of Native Education, which in 1964 became the Department of African Education within the Ministry of Education. But the controversy continued, centering on whether, and the extent to which, "native education" should depart from offering industrial and other training that would suit Africans only for a servile role in the colonial scheme. The missionaries, especially the Methodists, maintained their pressure on the government to remove restrictions on African education, and won the substantial agreement of the Kerr Commission (under Sir Alexander Kerr) in 1952. But the administration continued to devise ways to curtail Africans' access to education, including attempting, beginning around 1970, to force missionaries out of operating schools. The stance of the white minority government on this issue was instrumental in turning schools into fertile recruiting grounds for the freedom fighters once the *chimurenga* flared in 1972.

From a modern, Western perspective, the advantages and benefits of Western-style education are self-evident. Also, the initiative by some African groups to provide such education for African youths in the face of the white administration's reluctance is evidence that those groups also recognized the benefits. Tsitsi Dangarembga's novel *Nervous Conditions* (1989) provides a reliable representation of Africans' attitude toward Western education. But while the novel demonstrates its great potential as a guarantor of prestige and the good life (in the example of Babamukuru, the London-educated uncle of the heroine), it also illustrates the devastating alienating (and disorienting) effects of such an education on sensitive African youths like Nyasha, his anglicized daughter. Even in the case of the novel's heroine, Tambudzai, one of the major results of her increased access to Western education (and the lifestyle associated with it) is her growing disdain for her mother's traditional way of life and her disgust with the homestead where she was raised, in preference for her life with Babamukuru and his wife Maiguru at the mission school he heads.[19]

Tambu's disgust with her mother's lifestyle is consistent with the attitude the missionaries inculcated in their students toward traditional ways. They indoctrinated the students into believing that traditional habits were filthy, and that they must abandon them for Western ones:

> Most African students attending mission and state schools from the late 1920s onward found themselves in a world where they were encouraged to think of themselves as the favored clean among the "great unwashed" of the uneducated and unconverted. Many Zimbabwean activists and writers prominent after WWII were young children attending school during these years and their writings have provided rich autobiographical testimony regarding the ways in which educational discourse about hygiene and manners became integral to a sense of self for many elite Africans, about how hygiene as a form of discipline shaped racial identity in colonial society.[20]

An African graduate of one such school recalls a song he and his fellow pupils were made to sing every morning when they went to the stream to bathe: "We are the newcomers, / We are the newcomers, / We are dirty, / We are dirty, / We do not know how to wash ourselves. / We have not acquired education."[21]

Mission education thus taught Africans to be embarrassed by their traditional ways, and especially by such cultural practices and identifying marks as filed gaps in their front teeth or totally pulled teeth, and tribal facial markings; they came to resent their parents and elders for thus disfiguring them. The attitude was so prevalent among the youth that even the Department of Native Administration felt obliged to warn at some point, "We must not look back on our primitive parents and say with a broken spirit "Ah look at the dirt and old dilapidated huts in which they live." It is really wrong for us to say such things."[22]

Developments After Independence

On gaining independence the Zimbabwe government set about undoing the damage that decades of neglect and abuse had inflicted on African lives. One of its main focuses was education. Shortly after it took power it introduced free primary education and made secondary education easily affordable. School desegregation followed a year later. Furthermore, the government replaced the Eurocentric curriculum with one more relevant to the African experience and established teacher training institutions. As a result of these measures enrollment in primary and secondary schools rose dramatically.

University education had been available within the country since 1957, during the federation period. The institution that provided it, the University College of Rhodesia and Nyasaland, was sited in Salisbury (now Harare). Following the practice in other British colonies, it was linked to London University, but its medical school, which was established in 1963, was affiliated with the University of Birmingham. In 1964, after the federation broke up, it became the University College of Rhodesia. Six years after UDI, in 1971, the college dropped its affiliation with London and became the University of Rhodesia, awarding its own degrees rather than London University ones. At independence in 1980 it changed its identity once more, becoming the University of Zimbabwe, and in 1988 it welcomed its first black principal, Walter J. Kamba.

The institution remained a bastion of integrity throughout the years of repressive white minority rule and through the period of the *chimurenga,* maintaining its ideological and academic autonomy, as well as an integrated community of faculty and students, in spite of the racist policies of Ian Smith's Rhodesian Front regime. It also offered a platform for the expression of opinion critical of the minority regime.

From a full-time student enrollment of 70 at its inauguration in 1957, the university's student population had risen to about 10,000 by 2000, with a faculty numbering over 500. Today the faculties (colleges) include arts, commerce, law, education, engineering, medicine, science, social studies, and veterinary science. In 1982 the P. R. Williams Commission of Inquiry appointed to look into the university's affairs recommended that a second campus be set up to specialize in education and/or science and technology. In the process of implementing that recommendation, the government decided in 1989 to establish a second university instead, to be located at Bulawayo. The new university, the National University of Science and Technology, Bulawayo, began operating in temporary quarters in 1991, with P. M. Makhurane as its first vice-chancellor, and moved to its permanent site in August 1998.

In January 1992 the Zimbabwe National Council for Higher Education granted a charter to the United Methodist Church to establish what was to become the first United Methodist–related university in Africa, and Zimbabwe's first private university. In March 1992 instruction began in temporary buildings in Mutare, with forty students in the faculties of theology and agriculture and natural resources, and sixteen teaching and administrative staff members. Africa University officially opened in April 1994, and in December of the same year it graduated its first class of twenty-seven. By 1995 its enrollment had increased to 125 students, and in 1996 the university added two new faculties: the faculty of management and administration and the faculty of education.

Complementing the aforementioned institutions of higher learning are technical colleges in Harare, Bulawayo, Gweru, Chinhoyi, Mutare, and Kwe Kwe, in addition to several agricultural colleges.

Western Impact on Lifestyle

The European impact on African lifestyles took different forms, the change in the manner and content of education being only one. Another was the creation of a new attitude toward the body. The traditional African is typically free of obsession about the body, or embarrassment about it, and pays more attention to being comfortable in the prevailing climate and environment than to concealing as much of the body as possible from view. That is why traditional casual attires were scanty as a rule, covering little more than the genitals. After the establishment of colonialism, the administration granted extensive land holdings to the missions, who thus became landlords to large populations of Africans, among them nonconverts. The missions were thus able to dictate dress habits to their tenants, and the Africans for their part had no option but to submit to those dictates if they wanted access to the fertile lands under the missions' control.

In Chapter 7 the missions' use of "Jeanes teachers" in changing Africans' lifestyles was touched on. These teachers inspected Africans' homes and surroundings to ensure that they complied with Europeans' notions of tidiness and cleanliness, and often took matters into their own hands to effect their desires. These agents of westernization were so persuaded of the superiority of their Western models that they habitually referred to African customs as primitive and "filthy," including such practices as eating with the fingers from communal bowls. The brash manner in which these teachers, both male and female, intruded into Africans' private lives generated considerable resentment against them, to the extent that African elders often forbade their youths to attend mission schools.

Women's Clubs and Urban Survival

The Ruwadzano movement that began in Christian mission circles in the 1920s, apart from serving the missions in their evangelization, eventually became a means through which African women could come together for collective social and political action. Lay women borrowed a leaf from the Ruwadzanos and began to form social clubs in the 1940s. These clubs constituted a support group that offered urban women a replacement for the kind of mutual aid village women could count on in times of crisis. Following is an example of how urban women substitute for the care and advice the *ambuya* (grandmothers) used to provide.

A Baby Shower

The baby shower is a social event that is popular among the well educated and successful professional women in the cities, although it is not their exclusive preserve. Close to the time of her delivery, an expectant mother arranges such a party and invites her friends. A friend or friends might also take the initiative to organize the party. In either case, the mother-to-be's friends are all invited, and the occasion usually takes the form of a costume party at her house. Because it is for women only the invitees seize the opportunity to be free and uninhibited in a way they cannot be in mixed company. They wear provocative dresses, or go in demure ones but pack a more suggestive change of clothing to don on arrival. The hostess herself dresses accordingly, sometimes helping the spirit of the festivities by painting risqué motifs on her pregnant belly.

When the party begins, the guests take turns introducing themselves, making up naughty names for the occasion and provoking hearty laughter with their jokes. Next, the mother-to-be opens the presents that the guests have brought, an activity that is something of a performance. Before she opens each one she must guess what it is, and if she guesses wrong she must do a dance for the group. After the first wrong guess, the considerate rules permit her to appoint a designated dancer to substitute for her. The presents are usually items the new mother will need after the baby's arrival. The presents having all been opened, the guests eat the feast that their hostess has prepared.

Following the eating (and drinking), general dancing ensues; some of the women assume male roles in naughty couple dances, enlivened with much bumping and thrusting. After that interlude, some serious business follows: a professional nurse or midwife, who is there for the purpose, gives practical advice to the expectant mother. That brings the function to an end.

Through the device of a baby shower, therefore, the urban woman has access to the advice and help the village woman used to receive from her father's sister and the older women of the extended family, and even to the practical, material help (including medicine) that they also provided.[23]

A Modern Shona Funeral

The following description of a Shona funeral demonstrates, among other things, the persistence of the hold of tradition, even on people who have effectively left the village behind and have become successful in the new dispensation. The deceased, a successful businessman who had spent his last years in the capital as well as in European cities, died from AIDS. He had elected to spend his last days in his home village and to be buried with his ancestors. During the days before the funeral, mourners have assembled in the home of the deceased, including women known as the *varoora* (daughters-in-law) from his mother's village. She has achieved the honorific status of great aunt or "honorary man" in her village, and the *varoora* are there to offer her support and to do the cooking for the funeral. Because the deceased had lived a good life and has left survivors, the occasion is not too gloomy; there is in fact a feeling of celebration and room for some lightheartedness. While the mourners sing traditional songs, the *varoora*, who are strangers in the village and can hide behind their anonymity, poke fun at them and even lampoon the dead man's known weakness for women.

On the eve of the burial, the female close relatives—mother, sisters, wife, and girlfriends—sit around the coffin and sing, cry, and dance. At dawn on the burial day, four days after the death, the mother of the dead man walks around her front yard calling his name and mournfully asking him to rise with the dawn. After the sun has risen, her people lead her back inside and offer her warm water to bathe herself.

The procession to the grave and the burial follow the traditional form. A light rain falls on the mourners as they return from the grave site, which they interpret as the ancestors' contribution to the occasion, something to wash the footprints of the deceased from this earth and smooth his passage to the next life.[24]

One final observation on the ways in which traditional practices have had to adjust to new times. Because of the mobility that the new times make possible and the frequent necessity for people to travel far away from home, it does happen sometimes that a person dies in a foreign land and his or her body cannot be repatriated. The Shona practice in such circumstances is to wait for a period of up to several years until the family is satisfied that the body will never return. Then they go through the usual burial ceremonies, accompanied by the usual mourning, just as though the body were present, the only difference being the burial of a goat's head in the grave in place of the corpse.[25]

NOTES

1. Charles Bullock, *The Mashona (The Indigenous Natives of S. Rhodesia)* (1928; reprint, Westport, CT: Negro Universities Press, 1970), 195, 196.

2. Ibid., 199–200.
3. Solomon M. Mutswairo, *Mapondera, Soldier of Zimbabwe* (Washington, DC: Three Continents Press, 1978), 1–3.
4. Ibid., 4.
5. Bullock, 201.
6. Timothy Burke, *Lifebuoy Men, Lux Women: Commodification, Consumption, and Cleanliness in Modern Zimbabwe* (Durham: Duke University Press, 1996), 30.
7. Ibid., 29.
8. Bullock, 251.
9. Ibid., 206.
10. Ibid.
11. A. C. Hodza and G. Fortune, comps. and eds., *Shona Praise Poetry* (Oxford: Oxford University Press, 1979), 26.
12. Ibid., 26.
13. Bullock, 210.
14. Ibid., 214.
15. Ibid., 223–26.
16. Ibid., 220–21.
17. Ibid., 226–27.
18. John S. Mbiti, *African Religions and Philosophy* (New York: Praeger, 1969), 150.
19. Tsitsi Dangarembga, *Nervous Conditions* (Seattle, WA: Seal Press, 1989), 140.
20. Burke, 40.
21. Ibid., 41.
22. Ibid.
23. Sekai Nzenza-Shand, *Songs to an African Sunset: A Zimbabwean Story* (Melbourne: Lonely Planet Publications, 1997), 160.
24. Ibid., 21.
25. Ibid., 186.

8

Music and Dance

IN ZIMBABWE, as in other parts of Africa, music is an ever-present feature of daily life. The people hold music in such high regard that they claim supernatural origins for it. The ability to play the mbira (the most popular instrument in Zimbabwe), they say, is a gift from the ancestors, who taught it to the first mbira player in a dream. Those whom the ancestors favor are also recognized by their skillful mbira playing and dancing, especially in connection with *bira* ceremonies. In fact, the crucial role music plays in these ceremonies, in which it is the means of summoning the spirit to possess its medium, is a confirmation of its centrality to Shona well-being, because that well-being depends on ascertaining the pleasure of the ancestors and maintaining constant contact with them. Furthermore, music—singing, drumming, clapping, and playing a variety of musical instruments—is the constant companion of people either at work or engaged in other activities: on their farms, herding their cattle, threshing and grinding, or walking to the market.

Traditionally, group singing was a unifying force when the people were engaged in collective endeavors, preparing for war, for example, or working together at harvest. Music accompanies rituals (including the installations of chiefs, worshiping and consulting the ancestors, and celebrating births, marriages, and funerals) and features at official functions of chiefs, who maintain drum sets in their homes for the purpose. Folktales incorporate songs as refrains and sung incantations, or as means of advancing the action, and often songs that entertain and ease the strain of work are risqué and targeted at social offenders and domestic enemies, thus functioning as a means of social control and of reinforcing group mores.

Archeological finds of musical iron bells in several Zimbabwe sites (as well as in the Shaba region of the Democratic Republic of the Congo) point to the antiquity of instrumental music in the area, and it is safe to assume that the inhabitants of the region resorted to some form of musical expression as soon as they learned to do so in speech, perhaps even before that. As far as the Shona are concerned, scholars speculate that their practice of yodeling suggests influences from Pygmies, who lived in the area before the Bantu-speakers arrived, and also point to similarities between Shona and San tonal harmonies as further evidence of the relationship, because of the closeness of the harmonics of a musical bow and the structure of the Shona mbira.[1]

The history of Zimbabwe is a record of several immigrations of different groups, each bringing its own peculiar musical tradition and instruments. For example, the single and double iron bells, which are used here as elsewhere, are presumed to have originated in West Africa, from where their use spread to western Central Africa during the Iron Age and later to Zimbabwe and the Zambezi River Valley. Iron prongs have been discovered in Zimbabwe, and the forerunners of the mbira, the instrument most closely identified with Zimbabwe music, are believed to have entered the region beginning in the seventeenth century. Lamellophones with iron keys spread northward from the Zambesi Valley and have evolved over the ages: those that travelers carried with them on their journeys became smaller, while others were modified in other ways in accordance with their new environment and employment. By the first half of the twentieth century their current dimensions and characteristics had become fixed.

MUSICAL INSTRUMENTS

Mbira

The mbira is a lamellophone consisting of a sounding board on which are mounted several metal *lamellae* (prongs, usually iron); it is familiar to many people in the West as the thumb piano. The performer plays the instrument by plucking its iron prongs with the thumbs and forefingers. In one shape or another it is ubiquitous in Africa, but nowhere is its use as prominent as in Zimbabwe, where it is the centerpiece of Shona music. The board is usually solid, an exception being the hollow Korekore *hera*, which is usually about $7\frac{1}{2}$ inches (19 cm) wide, and slightly larger from front to back. Before the arrival of Europeans, blacksmiths made the prongs from smelted iron; now they are manufactured from nails or wires (from bicycle and car seats) that have been pounded flat. One end of these prongs is attached to the board, and each piece is thence secured over a metal bridge such that the free end is elevated, ready for plucking. The longer the free end extends over the bridge, the lower the sound it produces, and the prongs can be tuned by being slid back or forth over the bridge. In arrangement the longest pieces occupy the center, the length diminishing progressively toward the two edges. Large gourds are used as resonators to increase the volume during ritual and public performances. Rattles made from snail shells or bottle caps are sometimes placed in the hollow of the *hera* and related types of mbira to produce a buzzing sound. With the *mbira dzavadzimu* (the mbira dedicated to the ancestors) the rattles are outside the board, while the *njeri* type has them on the resonator.

Mbira is almost synonymous with music in Zimbabwe, and, since the term denotes the instrument as well as the music, it is what automatically comes to mind when discussion turns to the subject. According to one scholar, "As the piano provides a conceptual basis for the Western musical system, so the mbira provides a conceptual basis for the Shona, which is primarily an improvisational tradition, with both vocal and instrumental performances based on recurring harmonic and rhythmic cycles."[2] Whereas in other parts of Africa an mbira-like instrument might feature singly and in a minor role in an ensemble of other instruments, or mbira of different ranges might be used together, Shona mbira ensembles usually comprise instruments of the same type, and on occasions an mbira ensemble might include fifteen or more instruments. Perhaps because the mbira plays a central role in communions with ancestors and in other Shona religious ceremonies, the Shona consider mbira players to be the most accomplished musicians, and a master mbira artist is given the title *gwenyambira*.

Types of Mbira   Chief among mbira types is the *mbira dzavadzimu*, the mbira of the ancestral spirits, which is also known as *huru* (or *nhare*), meaning "iron." It features twenty-two or more wide keys, which the player plucks with the forefinger of the right hand and both thumbs. Its resonance especially suits it both to the meditative mood of a seance and to spirited dancing. The Shona associate this type of mbira primarily with the Zezuru people.

The Korekore mbira—*hera, munyonga, matepe*, or *madhebhe*—has about twenty-nine narrow keys and is played with both thumbs and both forefingers. It produces faster and lighter music and more complex rhythms than the *dzavadzimu*'s, and its bass notes are lower. The *njari*, which came from the Zambezi River Valley in the 1700s, is used in rituals concerning tutelary spirits, but it also accompanies nonritual singing. The *karimba* (or *kalimba*), which is the smallest type and which has no ritual functions, is believed to be the one from which the others developed. It is often used to instruct beginners. The *nyunga nyunga* of the Manyika culture is a type of *karimba*, and is played with both thumbs and the right forefinger.

Marimba

The marimba is a sort of xylophone with wooden keys suspended over resonators of different types. Sometimes these are gourds, and sometimes they are tubes capped at the bottom but with side holes covered by skin or some other membrane. During play, this covering vibrates and lends resonance to the sound, adding a buzzing effect to the characteristic deep sound of the marimba. The preferred wood for the keys is that of the *mwenje* tree, whose hardness lends particular resonance to the keys. When an ensemble of eight marimba players (the usual number) performs the intricate, lively, interwoven music of the instrument, the urge to dance is irresistible.

The marimba is a late arrival in Zimbabwe: its introduction occurred in the early 1960s at the Kwanongoma College of Music in Bulawayo, which was founded to teach European as well as African music. The original type, the soprano, tenor, and baritone, has a range of two octaves of diatonic keys, corresponding to the diatonic white keys of the piano, and, in addition, the F-sharp key. Credit for the invention of the other type, the bass marimba, belongs to Dumisani Maraire, who developed it in Seattle, Washington, in the 1970s, when he began teaching music there. As a result of its popularization by the Kwanongoma College, the marimba has become a familiar musical instrument in secondary schools, urban centers, and resorts.

Drums

The Shona sometimes use various types of drums (*ngoma*) to accompany mbira, especially of the *hera* type. The drums range in size from about eight inches to four feet in height, and are used in ensembles of two or more, and with rattles, but they are sometimes used by themselves to accompany singing. The traditional drum ensemble features three types of instrument. In all cases one end is covered with skin fastened to the body with pegs and strings, and the other end is open. Traditionally, the skin used was from the zebra or a water lizard, but nowadays cowhide is prevalent. The smallest drum is the *mhito*, which the player often beats with sticks to provide the basic rhythm. The largest, the *dandi*, is played with both hands, with sticks, or a combination of both. The third type is the *mutumba*; it is waist high and produces a low-pitched sound. To play it, performers straddle it as it lies on the ground. They may also sit and support the drum with their knees, or stand it upright and play it while standing.

Another percussion instrument is the *mujeje*, thought to be the oldest instrument of its type, because it is simply the exfoliated rock to be found widespread in the countryside, and which gives a resonant sound when struck.

Wind Instruments

Zimbabwe wind instruments include flutes, pipes, and horns. There are double and single flutes, both of them blown from the side. The double flute combines low-pitched (bass) and high-pitched (treble) companion pipes. In addition, there are end-blown flutes made of dried fruit pods, bamboo flutes, and hand-flutes. Other wind instruments are the traditional hunting pipe, the panpipe made of several bamboo tubes (as many as eight) of different lengths secured with strings and wax, and animal horns. The panpipe is popular among the northern Shona, who use it in groups for entertainment. The horns are primarily for communicating codes, but are also used in traditional religious observances, a use that some modern churches have adopted.

Strings

Zimbabwe music features various stringed instruments, among them different types of bows, while playing which the musicians often also whistle and sing. The most popular of these, especially with herdboys, is the mouth-harp (*chipendani*), a bent stave with two ends that hold a taut string in tension. The player holds the harp in his mouth and plucks the string with the fingers of both hands, while using the mouth to control the tones. In response to modernity, in particular the replacement of cattle herding by schooling, the use of the mouth-harp has declined, giving way to banjos and homemade guitars.

Rattles

The *hosho* is a hand-held rattle made by filling a tin can or the hollowed-out inside of a gourd with hard seeds. An important member of the mbira and marimba ensembles, *hosho* are used in pairs to mark the beat of the music. In addition to accompanying marimba and mbira ensembles, including the *dzavadzimu*, the *hosho* also accompanies singing. Although simple in appearance, the instrument calls for some skill and practice in order to be played effectively and well, and because of its beat-regulating role, some commentators go as far as to assign to the *hosho* the central role in the ensembles in which it features. Other types of *hosho* are the leg rattles *magagada, majaka,* and *madare* (bells), *magavhu,* and *tswawo.* The *madare* is made up of bells, the *magavhu* comprises up to three gourds on each leg, while the *tswawo* can combine as many as eight smaller gourds on each leg. The Ndebele leg rattle is called the *mahlwayi.* Leg rattles are typically worn by dancers on their ankles.

SINGING

Singing is pervasive among the different cultures. People sing as they relax, walk, work, and worship. The Shona distinguish between traditional songs—*nyizo dzepasi* (meaning "songs of the earth"), which accompany play, hunting, funerals, and rituals directed toward *midzimu* (tutelary spirit) and *mashave*—and modern ones—*chimanjemanje.* Rituals generally incorporate traditional songs that came down from the ancestors and that have been in use from time immemorial. The singing of these songs, as well as dancing, usually occupies the night before a ritual ceremony. In the case of funerals old men sit with the corpse inside the hut and sing these songs, while the younger people sing and dance to modern songs outside. The next day the funeral party sings special funerary songs, *ngondo* and *dendende,* as they convey the body to the grave. The later ritual of *kurova guva,* which releases the spirit of the dead from the grave and permits it to go in search of a medium, also involves a night of singing and dancing. The singing continues as the celebrants go to the grave at daybreak, when they clean around the grave, and during the sacrifice that concludes the ceremony.

In traditional singing the mbira accompanies the singers, providing the harmony and rhythm for their songs. Mbira players must themselves be accomplished singers, for their singing ability, including the ability to yodel, to lead in the call-and-response format, and to improvise, is one of the skills on which people base their assessment of mbirists' overall merit. Whether accompanied or not, however, songs retain their harmonies. In the call-and-response format the lead singer may vary the lead, but the responses are consistent.

Modern singing, as in school and churches, features songs that are either European or European-influenced. An example is the European-influenced hybrid that has resulted from the intrusion of urban life into the villages, the *makwaya,* "syncopated choral pieces developed by black South African composers."[3] This genre, which combines European harmony and African fast dancing and call-and-response patterns, is especially popular among the young.

The *chimurenga* songs that rallied the combatants' spirits and also strengthened the resolve of the noncombatants during the struggle for independence now find employment, along with traditional war songs, at sports matches and political rallies.

MUSIC AND RITUALS

In addition to playing a central role in Zimbabwe rituals, in particular in *bira* but also in others, like funerals, music also features prominently in rain-making ceremonies. In all cases the featured instrument is the mbira, but the *bira* remains its special arena.

GENDER AND MUSIC

There are no fixed gender roles in music. Women used to do the *mafuwe*, one of the rainmaking dances, but now men also participate, especially when the performance is for entertainment. Also, while traditionally only men played the mbira, now women also do; similarly, although men predominate in the ranks of drum players, here too women have made inroads.

THE EUROPEAN INFLUENCE

The development of Zimbabwe music can be seen in three periods: the pre-European period characterized by traditional, indigenous music; the European-influenced (colonized) period, with its introduction of European music and the deployment of Shona music in the political struggle; and the period of the *chimurenga*.

European influence on Zimbabwe music dates back to at least 1872, when Karl Mauch made the first attempt to reduce it to notation. Subsequently, the influence was strongest during the colonial period, resulting in the near demise of traditional music during the twentieth century, especially in the central plateau (the stronghold of the Europeans). It also suffered because of the preference for European music in schools and churches, which discouraged African music in favor of European hymns that have been translated into local languages. Church hymns and choral music, with its four-part harmonies, replaced communal singing, and an emphasis on meter replaced the African preference for rhythm and polyphony, the mixing of several melodies. Finally, the military was another establishment whose preference for modern Western marches worked to the further detriment of traditional genres, for example the war songs.

The new music also enforced a modified concept of what was acceptable. Whereas in the past every singer sang in his or her own way, now there was an imposed uniform standard, and those who could not measure up to it were looked upon as incompetent. Traditional singing dynamics and embellishments were not spared. Dancing was discouraged, and new rules for modulating the voice came into force. The new culture also severely restricted the use of traditional instruments. Catholics, for example, frowned on the use of the mbira in church ceremonies because they regarded it as heathen, and forbade their adherents to play other native musical instruments, whether mbira, drums, rattles, or flutes. But in the end these developments failed to stop the people from imposing their stamp on the new hymns and songs. Paul Simon's *Graceland* album testifies to the resilience and persistence of the distinctive character of traditional music, in a salutary marriage of traditional and Western structures and harmonies.

MUSIC AND THE UPRISING

The armed struggle against colonialism, known as the *chimurenga*, made widespread use of the mbira, the symbol of Shona identity. *Chimurenga* music developed at the urging of the freedom fighters, who challenged the musicians to turn away from their imitation of such Western performers as Elvis Presley, the Beatles, and the Rolling Stones, and instead aid the struggle with their music. The resulting new revolutionary songs often simply substituted new lyrics for old church tunes, and at times altered the meaning of Christian texts and references in the service of the cause. Also, as part of the revolutionary strategy, the musicians redirected the barbs of traditional songs, from being aimed at unjust chiefs to condemning the Smith regime, and they also applied traditional war and hunting songs to the black-white conflict.

Chimurenga songs pervaded all styles of music—*makwaya, jocho, jiti,* Ndebele songs, mbira songs, modern songs, and church hymns. In the 1970s, a freedom fighters' radio station located in Mozambique broadcast programs to counter those of the Rhodesia Broadcasting Corporation, and local artists recorded oppositional songs in Shona for sale. The revolution found new uses for the old songs which had fallen into disfavor under white pressure, thus achieving the cultural end of reinvigorating a valuable traditional means of expression.

After independence, *chimurenga* music broadened to include praises of the leaders, and broadcasts on Radio Zimbabwe expanded their scope to embrace other music, Ndebele, Western, and so forth. The College of Music in Harare, which had earlier taught serious European music, also began to teach Shona music.

Recently, hybrid forms of music have developed, such as the *makwaya* (choir), a South Africa choral singing style (frequently accompanied by marching) that became popular before the 1950s. Dance styles emerged in the 1970s, including the *jocho* (with little European influence), and the much preferred *jiti* or *jez* (jazz) which combines African drumming, call and response, and European-style harmonics. The influence of independence is also apparent in the curriculum of the Kwanongona College of Music, which trains African school teachers. It teaches the mbira and xylophones. Different Christian denominations make different allowances for tradition. The Church Music Service (Methodist) encourages traditional music in church services and organizes workshops to encourage African composers. The Jews are even more liberal, permitting a whole range of traditional practices. On the other hand, the Vapostori (Apostolics) are far more conservative: while, unlike other sects, they permit polygamy, they do not tolerate the use of drums (or beer drinking).

Thomas Mapfumo and Chimurenga Music

Most famous among the *chimurenga* artists was Thomas Tafirenyika Mukanya Mapfumo (b. 1945). A musician, poet, and political activist/commentator, Mapfumo learned Shona music as a boy from his grandparents, and later adapted mbira music for the guitar for his first group, Acid Band, later renamed Blacks Unlimited. He started his career in the 1970s imitating Western rock and embracing Western culture, including its dress code: flared trousers, tight-fitting T-shirts, and platform shoes. Once he switched to *chimurenga* music, though, he also changed his dress and appearance, going on stage shirtless in a loincloth, and holding a ceremonial axe in one hand and the microphone in the other. At other times he performed wearing the black-and-white robes characteristic of spirit mediums.

Not particularly beloved of the Zimbabwean elite, he is the idol of the working and underprivileged people. For his part, he seeks to be inclusive in his music, using language that characterizes all Zimbabweans as a collective unit, and singing of reconciliation, social, political, and economic. He also urges the people to embrace and celebrate their culture. His songs were banned from the radio by the Smith government, but they could be sold on records because the recorded lyrics were sanitized, or veiled their true import. He was himself imprisoned for ninety days without trial in 1977.

Like most Zimbabweans, Mapfumo became disillusioned after independence, and he gave voice to his disappointment with the Mugabe regime in such albums as *Chamunorwa* (Corruption), which came out in 1990 and was banned from the state's media. He also favored Morgan Tsvangirai's Movement for Democratic Change in the 2000 elections,[4] further incurring the displeasure of the government.

THE MUSIC INDUSTRY

Radio and the electronic media have transformed the world into a global village, exposing Zimbabwe to bombardment with Western (American and European) pop music, as well as music from South Africa, Zaire, and West Africa. The Rhodesia Broadcasting Corporation began recording and broadcasting local music in the early 1950s. For commercials, it patronized enterprising young musicians who used locally made instruments in their imitation of Western performers. They soon graduated to playing at beer parties, urban hotels, and night clubs. By the 1970s they had become sophisticated enough to use foreign instruments and amplification, often paid for by patrons who took a cut of the bands' profits. Recordings of Shona songs also became popular. Nowadays in the cities, music comes blaring from shops, cars, and hand-held radios, and it is more likely to be reggae or *kwela* (a western African hybrid imported from South Africa). As a sign of the internationalization of Zimbabwe music, reggae superstar Bob Marley was part of the independence ceremonies in 1980, and Harare hosted Paul Simon's famous Graceland concert in 1987.

GIANTS OF MBIRA

Among the best known Zimbabwe musicians is Mondreck Muchena (d. 1995), known as the gentle giant of mbira. He was a member of the mbira ensemble Mhuri yekwaRwizi, and, later the leader of Mhuri yekwa-Muchena, which performed for the country's president and visiting dignitaries on state occasions. His three trips to Europe between 1984 and 1994 did much to popularize Zimbabwe music and the mbira on that continent. He also taught mbira playing, while also performing at *mapira* (*bira* sessions).

Stella Rambisai Chiweshe is perhaps the most famous of the female mbira performers today. Born in the late 1940s, she grew up about forty-five miles from Harare. She started learning to play the mbira in 1964, earning the disapproval of people who regarded women players of the instrument as loose. The year 1974 saw the recording of her first single, "Kawasha"; it was followed by twenty-four more in the next six years. In 1981 she joined the National Dance Company, with which she has traveled and performed abroad. In 1998 she joined Susana Baca and Tish Hinojosa in a Global Divas tour.[5] Another female performer is Benita Tarupiwa (b. 1971), who leads a group known as the Negombwe Mbira Group. It is based in Harare and performs traditional music and dance, as well as its own compositions. Her first recording, *Ndotamba Ndega*, was released in 1997.

Dumisani Maraire was born into a mbira-playing family in 1943, and he consequently learned the art at a young age from his uncles. He left the country during the period of political upheaval and went to the University of Washington at Seattle to teach Shona music and culture. He eventually returned to Zimbabwe to teach at the university. His best known recording is *Chaminuka*. He also collaborated with Ephat Mujuru on the album *Shona Spirit*.[6]

Ephat Mujuru (b. 1950), the son of a medium, learned to play the mbira very early, and performed at his first *bira* at the age of ten. He formed his first group, Chaminuka, in 1972, and played *chimurenga* music during the conflict. His song "Guruswa," composed and aired in the 1970s, was a veiled protest against white oppression. After independence he renamed the group Spirit of the People, and it made its first recording in 1981. He was instrumental in founding the National Dance Company of Zimbabwe and was the first African teacher at the Zimbabwe College of Music. In 1982 he came to the United States for university studies, winding up as a teacher of mbira and marimba at the University of Washington, Seattle. He has also performed at Carnegie Hall.[7]

Oliver "Tuku" Mtukudzi was inspired by Mapfumo. His popular Friday performances attract so-called Tuku Groupies, candle-waving dancers who raise their open palms skyward as a symbol of opposition to the regime. Andy Brown, whose "Nation of Thieves" has been banned from the media, is another popular performer who constitutes a thorn in the side of the Mugabe regime.

Other performers are the Bhundu Boys, whose specialty is *jit* music, a fast dance genre that gave its name to the popular film *Jit*; Black Umfolozi, an all-male internationally famous *a capella* singing group from Bulawayo, which was assembled in 1982 (it sings in both Ndebele and English, in a style called *imbube*);[8] the Four Brothers; New Black Montana; Robson Banda and the Black Eagles; Joseph Mutero; Steve Dyer; the Real Sounds of Africa; the Khiami Boys; the Ngwenya Brothers; Leonard Dembo; John Chibudura; and the Tembo Brothers.

DANCE

Nature and Significance of Dance

"To dance is human," but it is especially African.[9] Dance is always an important aspect of African rituals and social occasions, and Zimbabwe is no exception. We have already witnessed the close connection between ritual and dance in the example of the *mafuwe* dance as part of the *marenje* festival ritual (see chapter 5). As is the case elsewhere on the continent, dance and ritual are intimately connected. Dance also features prominently in Shona, and by extension Zimbabwe, cosmology, and is inseparable from the mores of the people.[10] In some places, the *jerusarema* dance is a feature of the funerary ceremony of the "mourning beer" (or *kurova guva*), and also of the *nhonga matomba*, which takes place one to three months after the burial of a deceased, as an expression of gratitude to the people who were at the grave site. The prohibition that women who are menstruating may not dance, and the other that a person who has been bereaved must not dance until after the first "mourning beer," attest to the ritual significance of the dance. The reason for the latter prohibition illustrates the cosmic power the people ascribe to dance. Its performance before the departed spirit has found safe anchor is capable of interfering with the spirit's voyage to the world of the ancestors; for that reason anyone who flouts that interdiction risks offending the ancestral spirits.

Dance has always pervaded Shona life: the mbira dance is believed to go back to the twelfth century, and the *jerusarema* to at least 1896,[11] but early students of Shona culture and society paid scant attention to it. Originally known as *mbende*, the *jerusarema* proved such an offense to the early missionaries that by 1910 they had placed a ban on it. The explanation for its name is an illustration of African resourcefulness in the face of European cultural persecution and of European naivete. Reportedly, after the missionaries instigated the ban on the dance, a Zezuru chief went to one of them and explained that the dance was actually in honor of the birth of the baby Jesus, whom the missionaries had spoken so much about. He had dreamt about all the chiefs singing and bearing gifts to Jerusalem to offer to the newborn Christ, and also about the Zezuru people singing and dancing. He wanted his people to be permitted to continue doing the dance in honor of Jesus. The missionaries' understanding of the story and misunderstanding of the chief's pronunciation of Jerusalem led to the new name *jerusarema*.[12] Another old dance, the *muchongoyo*, popular with the Nguni, is believed to have originated as a battle drill among the Zulu during the reign of King Chaka.

Types and Categories of Dance

As with traditional songs, which are attributed to the ancestors, the steps of traditional dances, especially sacred ones, are fixed and must be performed precisely. Innovations are permissible, but they must accord strictly with the received ones in spirit and values, even as they express new ideas and elements. In this way the dances remain dynamic rather than static, yet constant in spirit. Alongside the traditional dances are modern derivations of them that are put to uses different from the traditional, especially for public entertainment on modern stages and for limited durations, whereas traditional dances were in general performed in open-air arenas, in the round, and without time limitations. Furthermore, while in theory spirit possession was always a possibility in traditional dances, it is highly unlikely with the modern derivations.

There are as many as ten different dances in Zimbabwe society. Perhaps the most widespread is the mbira dance, which, as its name suggests, is danced to mbira music, and usually during *mapira*. It is believed to have originated among the Korekore of northern and western Mashonaland and to have spread from there to the central region of the country. Like the mbira, the *dinhe* is a Korekore dance that has the religious purpose of inducing possession, and is associated with planting and harvesting. The *shangara* belongs in central Mashonaland and has no religious function, while the *mbakumba* is danced by the Masvingo of southern Zimbabwe after the harvest and for entertainment. Other dances include the *chinyobera*, the *ngungu*, the *isitschikitsha*, the *amabhiza*, and the *ingquza*.[13]

Muchongoyo and Mbende/Jerusarema   The *muchongoyo*, which comes from the Chipinga district in Manicaland in the eastern part of Zimbabwe, and the *mbende/jerusarema* have the distinction of being features of the National Dance Company's repertory. The *muchongoyo* is a loud and spirited dance, marked by the resounding stamping of the feet that is an integral element of its performance. It originated with the Nguni as a variant of the Zulu *indlamu*, a military drill that honed precision action in regimental unison, but the Shona adopted it after migrant workers in South African mines brought it back home with them. The signature stick and shield that are part of the dancers' props attest to its military pedigree. The dancers' costumes are also distinctive, being traditionally lion skins, leopard skins, civet-cat skins, calf skin, and black and white ostrich feathers as the headdress.

Strictly a nighttime performance, *muchongoyo*'s accompaniment is limited to drums and other percussive instruments, and *hosho*.[14] Clubs are dedicated exclusively to its performance and popularization, the most prominent being the Simango Chihoo Family Muchongoyo Club.

The *mbende/jerusarema* belongs to the Mrewa district of eastern Mashonaland. Originally knowns as the *mbende* (meaning "mouse") among the Manyika to the east of the country, in Mashonaland it took the name *jocho*, but after the advent of Christian missionaries it became the *jerusarema*. The name *mbende* refers to the dancers' movements, which emulate the darting of the rodent. It originated as a military feint designed to lure the attacking enemy into reckless miscalculations, but these days one sees it performed in townships and beer halls, in funerary observances, and as a standard of the National Dance Company.

European and External Influences

As with many aspects of African life, colonial pressures forced structural transformations on the dance. Christian missionary prejudices imposed certain restrictions and modifications on African music and Africans' singing, and the dance, since it involved bodily expression, was even more subject to Christian sanctions. Tambu's description in *Nervous Conditions* of the singing and dancing with which Babamukuru's relatives welcomed him and his family back from Britain after an absence of five years is instructive. Unmarried uncles, cousins, and aunts, she says, played drums and *hosho*, sang, and danced in a circle, while others danced in the center of the circle. Tambu was herself moved to dance to the spirited and pulsating music, but she felt the censorship of the Christian establishment that was Babamukuru's sponsor and benefactor:

> My early childhood had been a prime time for dancing. Then I had used to amuse everybody by dropping my scholarly seriousness to twist and turn, and clap almost in time to the music. As I had grown older and the music had begun to speak to me more clearly, my movements had grown stronger, more rhythmical and luxuriant; but people had not found it amusing anymore, so that in the end I realized that there were bad implications in the way I enjoyed the rhythm. My dancing compressed itself into rigid, tentative gestures.[15]

Furthermore, even when they continue to be performed, and performed in accordance with traditional prescriptions, the venues for the performance, the occasions, and the purposes have changed. Traditional musicians, usually an mbira player and a drummer, are still in great demand, but their performing in a city night club, or even a city social gathering, cannot be the same as their summoning an ancestral visitation in a village *bira*. As with music, Christianity has been a particularly debilitating influence on the dance, which also struck the early missionaries as heathen and devilish. Even when missionary activities and proscriptions did not directly affect the dance, their detachment of Africans from their roots took a huge toll. At the very least, when people moved from their traditional hearths to the urban centers, with their pronounced Western tastes and influences, they most often left their traditional dances behind and took up such westernized substitutes as *jez* and *jiti*.

NOTES

1. John E. Kaemmer, "Music of the Shona of Zimbabwe," in Ruth M. Stone, ed., *Africa*, vol 1 of *The Garland Encyclopedia of World Music* (New York: Garland Publishing, 1998), 744–45.
2. Ibid., 747.
3. Paul F. Berliner, *The Soul of Mbira: Music and Traditions of the Shona People of Zimbabwe* (Chicago: University of Chicago Press, 1993), 26–27.
4. *The Guardian*, March 13, 2000.
5. The African Music Encyclopedia, "Stella Rambisai Chiweshe," www.africanmusic. org/artists/chiweshe.html.
6. Banning Eyre, "Shona Spirit: Passing on the Ancestral Music: An Interview with Ephat Mujuru," 2001, www.musicoftheworld.com/profile-ephat.html.
7. Ibid.
8. Deanna Swaney, *Zimbabwe, Botswana and Namibia* (Hawthorn, Australia: Lonely Planet Publications, 1999), 138.
9. Judith Lynne Hanna, *To Dance is Human: A Theory of Universal Communication* (Austin: U. of Teras Press, 1979).
10. For a good description of Zimbabwe dance, see Kariamu Welsh-Asante, *Zimbabwe Dance: Rhythmic Forces, Ancestral Voices. An Aesthetic Analysis* (Trenton, NJ: Africa World Press, 2000).
11. Ibid., 40.
12. Ibid., 44–45.
13. Ibid., 47.
14. Ibid., 79.
15. Tsitsi Dangarembga, *Nervous Conditions* (Seattle, WA: Seal Press, 1989), 42.

Glossary

a capella	style of singing without instrumental accompaniment
amadhlozi	Ndebele tribal spirit
binza	work the prospective groom's family performs on the prospective bride's father's farm as part of the marriage settlement
bira	session for consulting spirits through medium possession; pl. mapira
bopoto	a woman's public venting of a grievance against a powerful patriarch
Chaminuka	Shona great tribal spirit
chibaro	the enforced mine labor the white regime imposed on the African population in the 1960s.
chimurenga	war of liberation; the first started in 1896 and was crushed in 1897; the second began in 1966 and eventually led to the collapse of the white regime
chirema	expectant mother
chiremba	herbal doctors; pl. *zviremba*
chisi	sacred holiday in honor of ancestral spirits
daga	mud plaster used for building huts
dandaro	small-scale spirit possession session held in urban areas
dare	meeting place for men

difaqane	the crushing, referring to the Nguni-induced forced migrations of the 1820s to 1830s; see *mfecane*
dombo	prospective groom's envoy in marriage negotiations
Dzivaguru	Big Pool; one of Mwari's designations
gano	ceremonial axe carried by mediums and medicine men and women
hosho	hand-held rattle used in mbira and marimba ensembles
jerusarema	type of popular music and dance
jez	type of popular music and dance (based on jazz)
jiti	see *jez*
jocho	type of popular music and dance that emerged in the 1970s
kraal	village
kurova guva	third funerary ceremony (about a year after death)
kuviga	first burial ceremony immediately after death
kutamba guva	see *kurova guva*
kwela	Popular urban music
lobola	payment by the groom to the bride's family in compensation for the loss of her services
mambo	Shona for king
marenje	January festival to implore the tribal spirits to send rains for the growing season
mafuwe	a ritual dance by women during the *marenje*
masungiro	groom's expression of gratitude for a bride found to be a virgin at wedding
mbende	original name for *jerusarema*
mbira	musical instrument (thumb piano); also the music
mfecane	the scattering; the widespread population migrations caused by Chaka's military campaigns in the 1820s to 1830s; see *difaqane*
mharadzo	second burial ceremony (about a month after death)
mhondoro	tribal spirit
muchongoya	popular Nguni dance; believed to be derived from Zulu battle drill
mudzimu	ancestral spirit; pl. *midzimu, vadzimu*

Mutapa	Mutapa Mutota; also known as Mwene Mutapa, Monomotapa, etc.
Mwari	Shona Supreme Being
n'anga	medicine man or medicine woman (also *nganga*)
nechombo	*svikiro's* helper or acolyte
Nehanda	Nehanda Charwe Nyakasikana; woman medium with whom Sekuru Kaguvi instigated the first *chimurenga* in 1896
ngano	folktale
ngozi	vengeful spirit; cf. *shave*
nhaka	inheritance
roora	see *lobola*
Rozvi (Rozwi)	Shona state that thrived in the late 17th century
Ruwadzano	women's fellowship clubs formed in Methodist churches in the 1920s
sadza	stiff maize porridge; the Shona staple
svikiro	spirit medium
shave	vengeful spirit
uMlimu	Ndebele name for Mwari
vadzimu	see *mudzimu*
varoora	daughters-in-law
zimbabwe (n)	great stone house

Bibliography

Bâ, Mariama. *So Long a Letter*. London: Heinemann, 1981.

Barnes, Teresa. "'Am I a Man?': Gender and the Pass Laws in Urban Colonial Zimbabwe, 1930–80." *African Studies Review* 40, no. 1 (April 1997): 59–81.

Beach, D. N. *The Shona and Zimbabwe, 900–1850: An Outline of Shona History*. New York: Africana, 1980.

Bechky, Allen. *Adventuring in Southern Africa*. San Francisco: Sierra Club Books, 1997.

Berliner, Paul F. *The Soul of Mbira: Music and Traditions of the Shona People of Zimbabwe*. Chicago: University of Chicago Press, 1993.

Bullock, Charles. *The Mashona (The Indigenous Natives of S. Rhodesia)*. 1928. Reprint. Westport, CT: Negro Universities Press, 1970.

Burke, Timothy. *Lifebuoy Men, Lux Women: Commodification, Consumption, and Cleanliness in Modern Zimbabwe*. Durham, NC: Duke University Press, 1996.

Cheney, Patricia. *The Land and People of Zimbabwe*. New York: J. B. Lippincott, 1990.

Chinodya, Shimmer. *Can We Talk, and Other Stories*. Harare: Baobab Books, 1998.

———. *Dew in the Morning*. Gwelo, Zimbabwe: Mambo Press, 1982.

———. *Harvest of Thorns*. Oxford: Heinemann, 1991.

Chipamaunga, Edmund O.Z. *Chains of Freedom*. Harare: Zimbabwe Publishing House, 1998.

Dangarembga, Tsitsi. *Nervous Conditions*. First Pub., London: Women's Press, 1988. Seattle, WA: Seal Press, 1989.

Emecheta, Buchi. *The Slave Girl*. New York: George Braziller, 1977.

Gelfand, Michael. *Shona Religion, with Special Reference to the Makorekore*. Cape Town, Wynberg, and Johannesburg: Juta and Co., 1962.

Hodza, A. C., and G. Fortune, comps. and eds. *Shona Praise Poetry*. Oxford: Oxford University Press, 1979.

Hove, Chenjerai. *Bones*. Oxford: Heinemann, 1988.

———. *Shadows*. Oxford: Heinemann, 1991.

———. *Shebeen Tales*. Harare: Baobab Books, 1994.

Kaemmer, John E. "Music of the Shona of Zimbabwe." In Ruth M. Stone, ed., *Africa*. Vol. 1 of *The Garland Encyclopedia of World Music*. New York: Garland Publishing, 1998, 744–58.

Katiyo, Wilson. *Going to Heaven*. Harlow, Essex: Longman, 1979.

———. *A Son of the Soil*. London: Rex Collins, 1976.

Knipp, Thomas. "English-Language Poetry." In *A History of Twentieth-Century African Literatures*, ed. Oyekan Owomoyela. Lincoln: University of Nebraska Press, 1993, 105–37.

Krog, E. W., ed. *African Literature in Rhodesia*. Gwelo, Zimbabwe: Mambo Press, in association with the Rhodesia Literature Bureau, 1966.

Matambanadzo, Bella. "Cinema-Zimbabwe: The New Story Tellers." http://web.mit.edu/course/21/21f.853/africa-film/0315.html, October 1, 1996.

Mbiti, John S. *African Religions and Philosophy*. New York: Praeger, 1969.

McCrea, Barbara, and Tony Pinchuck. *Zimbabwe and Botswana: The Rough Guide*. London: Rough Guides Ltd., 1996.

Morgan, Robin, ed. *Sisterhood Is Global: The International Women's Movement Anthology*. New York: Anchor, 1984.

Moyo, A. "Religion and Political Thought in Independent Zimbabwe." In C. Hallencreutz and A. Moyo, *Church and State in Zimbabwe*. Gweru, Zimbabwe: Mambo Press, 1988.

Muchena, Olivia N. "Zimbabwe: It Can Only Be Handled by Women." In *Sisterhood Is Global: The International Women's Movement Anthology*, ed. Robin Morgan. New York: Anchor, 1984, 752–55.

Mungazi, Dickson A. *To Honor the Sacred Trust of Civilization: History, Politics, and Education in Southern Africa*. Cambridge, MA: Schenkman Publishing Co., 1983.

Mungoshi, Charles L. *Waiting for the Rain*. London: Heinemann, 1975.

Museum for African Art. *In the Presence of Spirits: African Art from the National Museum of Ethnology, Lisbon*. Published in conjunction with an exhibition of the same title organized by the Museum for African Art, New York, in cooperation with the National Museum of Ethnology, Portuguese Institute of Museums, Ministry of Culture, Lisbon, Portugal, and presented in New York from September through December 2000.

Mutswairo, Solomon M. *Mapondera, Soldier of Zimbabwe*. Washington, DC: Three Continents Press, 1978.

Myambo, Malissa Tandiwe. "Deciduous Gazettes." In *Opening Spaces: An Anthology of Contemporary African Women's Writing*, ed. Yvonne Vera. Oxford: Heinemann, 1999, 14–42.

Nair, Supriya. "Melancholic Women: The Intellectual Hysteric(s) in *Nervous Conditions.*" *Research in African Literatures* 26, no. 2 (Summer 1995): 130–39.

Nel, Karen. "Headrests and Hairpins Signifying More than Status." In *Hair in African Art and Culture.* Published in conjunction with an exhibition of the same title presented by the Museum for African Art, New York, February 9–May 28, 2000, 151–59.

Nzenza-Shand, Sekai. *Songs to an African Sunset: A Zimbabwean Story.* Melbourne: Lonely Planet Publications, 1997.

Palmer, Robin, and Isobel Birch. *Zimbabwe: A Land Divided.* Oxford: Oxfam, 1992.

Rasmussen, R. Kent, and Steven C. Rubert. *Historical Dictionary of Zimbabwe.* 2nd ed. Metuchen, NJ: Scarecrow, 1990.

Reynolds, Pamela. *Traditional Healers and Childhood in Zimbabwe.* Athens: Ohio University Press, 1996.

Samkange, Stanlake John Thompson. *African Saga: A Brief Introduction to African History.* Nashville: Abingdon Press, 1971.

Swaney, Deanna. *Zimbabwe, Botswana and Namibia.* Hawthorn, Australia: Lonely Planet Publications, 1999.

Vera, Yvonne. *Butterfly Burning.* New York: Farrar, Straus and Giroux, 2000.

———, ed. *Opening Spaces: An Anthology of Contemporary African Women's Writing.* Oxford: Heinemann, 1999.

Vogel, Joseph O. *Great Zimbabwe: The Iron Age in South Central Africa.* 2 Vols. New York: Garland, 1994.

Welsh-Asante, Kariamu. *Zimbabwe Dance: Rhythmic Forces, Ancestral Voices. An Aesthetic Analysis.* Trenton, NJ: Africa World Press, 2000.

Young, Eric. "Zimbabwe." In *Microsoft Encarta Africana.* Microsoft Corporation, 1999.

Index

About the Author

OYEKAN OWOMOYELA is a Ryan Professor of African Literature at the University of Nebraska, Lincoln.